Your Life Is A Story

God Loves Every Page of Your Life

YOUR LIFE IS A STORY

God Loves Every Page of Your Life

Dr. Frank McMeen

Copyright ©2025 by Dr. Frank McMeen

All rights reserved. No part of this book may be reproduced or utilized in any form or by any means, electronic or mechanical, including photocopy, recording, or by an information storage and retrieval system, without permission in writing from the publisher.

ISBN: 979-8-9896268-4-7

Printed and bound in the United States of America by Ingram Lightning Source

Edited by: Jacque Hillman, Kim T. Stewart, Katie Gould
Layout and design by: Kim T. Stewart
Cover: Photo by Frank McMeen; design by Kim T. Stewart
Chapter art by: Frank McMeen

The HillHelen Group LLC
470 North Parkway, Suite C
Jackson, TN 38305

The HillHelen Group LLC
635 North 65th Place
Mesa, AZ 85205

(731) 394-2894
www.hillhelengrouppublishers.com
hillhelengroup@gmail.com

Dedication

This book is dedicated to two couples who continue to have a profound impact on my life.

Jamie and Scott Gatlin are spiritual mentors for me as I age. After I attended college with them, God brought them back into my life in a powerful way.

I worship at the Skyline Church because Scott stepped up to me on my first visit, placed his arm around me, and got right up in my face. Scott said, "Frank, you were brought here for a reason, and I think we need to pray about that." It became clear to me that he was right. Scott brought God up in my life at a bigger and stronger level. In my home during our small group Bible Studies, Scott challenged me to think more about the Spirit working in my life.

Jamie and Scott's family is impressive. You can see their impact on their kids and grandkids. Scott has opened my eyes to "see others through Jesus's eyes."

Freda and John Hall continue to be precious to me. They have been mentors since my college days, and I am a better person for having them in my life. John helped me grow professionally and personally. Freda helped me look the part before I was even invited to go to the next level professionally.

John took me around the country to sing in an a cappella group while I was in college. Three years of standing with seventy-five other singers on a stage showed me a world that I had never seen before. How else could I have been able to sing at the lighting of the national Christmas tree or at the Fourth of July celebration in Washington, DC, beneath the Washington Monument?

Thank you to Freda, John, Jamie, and Scott! I am a better person and Christian for having you in my life.

Tennyson said, "I am a part of all I have met," and these two couples have become dear to my heart and continue to help me try to be more like Jesus.

High Praise for
Your Life Is a Story

"From beginning to end in Frank McMeen's easily readable book, *Your Life is a Story*, the author opens our minds to compare our times and biblical times. With humor, self-effacing stories, and broad knowledge of the Old and New Testaments, the author reminds the reader of the wisdom in the Bible, especially the life of Jesus. His stories of family heroes and heroines and people we meet on life's journey leave no doubt that our decisions, words we say, and how we live are 'our life stories.'"

—Shirley C. Raines, president emeritus, University of Memphis

"Dr. Frank McMeen's latest book, *Your Life Is a Story*, is a wonderful and interesting collection of events and people in his life that shaped him into the person he is. Our careers, family upbringings, and religious traditions were similar, so I related to nearly every experience he shared. Though each life is unique, readers will find many familiar threads that invite connection and reflection. Certainly, one's life is a culmination of events and people that come into it. This book will undoubtedly bring to the reader's remembrance the many people and circumstances that influenced them and inspire deep gratitude. Dr. McMeen weaves timeless principles from God's Word and biblical characters into his narrative in such a way to illustrate that living a life with purpose is, and should be, the goal for all of us.

"The book is an easy read, perfect for two or three evenings or mornings. However, each chapter can stand alone, making it an excellent devotional tool for daily or weekly reading, whether individually or in a group setting."

—Ronnie Sarver, former president of Friendship Christian School and Ezell-Harding Christian School

"This book is a powerful reminder that every individual matters and that our lives are deeply connected. It also shows us a loving picture of God. My friend has captured this truth with clarity and heart, offering readers both inspiration and insight. A compelling and timely work—highly recommended."

—Dr. Wayne Scott, executive vice president of Bethel University

"Frank McMeen has been a positive presence in my life for almost forty years now. His transparent look at God's Word kicks over many theological rocks and confronts many sacred cows. Having been on a similar journey myself from legalism to a grace-filled life, I count it a joy to be with Frank on this journey to eternity with God. He is truly one of the good ones."

—Devin Pickard, minister and small business owner, Centerville, Tennessee

"Dr. Frank McMeen has shared stories that can make a difference in the lives of those who wish to pursue satisfying and extravagant lives—lives that are not dependent on wealth, prestige, or power. He compares the extravagance of God in His creation of you and me, describing the complexity of our eyes and the eloquent beauty of nature.

"Frank's stories of interesting people he has met, faraway places he has visited, and the wisdom of his parents and friends are intriguing. He shares his faith in God through his challenges and mountaintop experiences. He reminds us of the intriguing promise that, '. . . no eye has seen, nor ear heard, nor the heart of man imagined, what God has prepared for those who love him.' "

—Dr. Milton Sewell, president emeritus of Freed-Hardeman University

"If you want to be inspired and encouraged, read this book! As a Southern gentleman raised on a farm, Frank is a warm storyteller, sharing thoughts from the heart. His knowledge and use of the Bible helps explain God's truth in a way that is easy to understand. His experiences and vivid recollections are shared in a way that makes it feel like you are sitting on the porch listening to a trusted and wise friend."

—Dr. James Thomas, president of Columbia Academy in Columbia, Tennessee

"All the world loves a story, and in his third volume of master storytelling, Dr. Frank McMeen has again connected the greatest stories ever told—those of Jesus and the Bible—to the real, everyday life situations that define us.

"With his creative mind and compassionate heart, it is not Frank's intent to merely inform and entertain, but to inspire, to realize the gift God has given us every day to make a difference in the world, one person at a time, like Jesus! You are writing your own story, and what you write is up to you."

—Dr. Billy R. Smith, professor emeritus of Bible at Freed-Hardeman University, minister at Henderson Church of Christ

"Dr. Frank McMeen's life exemplifies a life dedicated to service to others. Frank's writings share his experiences in an entertaining and often humorous manner, while also providing a deeper meaning and often a life lesson. Those fortunate enough to know Frank and who are familiar with his adventures will feel as if he is telling his story directly to them."

—Bobby Walden, Community Foundation trustee

Finally, brothers,
whatever is true,
whatever is honorable,
whatever is just,
whatever is pure,
whatever is lovely,
whatever is commendable,
if there is any excellence,
if there is anything worthy of praise,
think about these things.

—Philippians 4:8 (ESV)

FOREWORD
Your Life Is a Story

Enthusiastically, and without reservation, I recommend this book. Each chapter begins with a story, one Frank experienced, and his application of sacred concepts.

IT IS ALL ABOUT RELATIONSHIPS... and the STORIES that define them. We think of our lives as one ongoing story. The Old and New Testaments are the story of God's relationship with mankind and the hope of eternity with Him.

When Dr. Frank McMeen enters a room, those present are greeted with a warm and welcoming smile, a firm handshake, a level gaze, and a confident, "Good morning! Great to see you!"

Frank is a God-fearing, multitalented, civic-minded visionary; a restorationist/preservationist; and a servant leader.

Before you continue reading this foreword, skip ahead to the author biography on Page 111 and read an abridged list of Frank's career and community contributions. Then we will give you a few insights into this extraordinary man, whom my wife Freda and I have known for fifty years, half a century.

* * *

In fall 1975, Frank came into our lives as a college freshman auditioning for a seventy-voice college choral ensemble I was conducting. For me, the A Cappella Singers were a musical vehicle for teaching young adults social, sacred, and life skills to help sustain them on their journey to eternity.

When we performed a musical program, the singing was just a small part. Afterwards, students were expected to talk with audience members. The goal was to give students opportunities to become citizens of the world and become closer to God. Students learned to be comfortable in the presence of adults.

We had a rare opportunity to sing in the Rotunda of the US Capitol Building with congressmen and many staff members in the audience. The students were comfortable, and Frank McMeen was among the most comfortable.

Frank's A Cappella Singers membership was remarkably unremarkable—meaning Frank made certain he covered the basics. He was on time, he learned his music, he took care of his tux, he learned how to knot a bow tie. He helped others in the group. He engaged with guests, and wrote the obligatory "Thank You" note for the night's lodging. Soon, Frank became THE student who delivered the recruiting invitation address at every concert. Freda taught a class in social skills. Frank owned the class content. Frank McMeen does not take shortcuts!

A career change took Freda and me to the Washington, DC, area. As a collegiate admissions officer, Frank traveled the nation. When in the Northeast, Frank always visited us in the Washington,

DC, area. Decades ago, Frank helped us plant a tree that still grows in that lawn.

Upon reflection, we know a half-century friendship would have various facets. Frank the student became vice president and chief fundraising officer for the college—by this time, university—and he invited us to return to lead again the A Cappella Singers.

Frank's career led him to become chief executive officer of a large non-profit organization. Frank called on the choral ensemble I was leading—twenty-five years after Frank was a member—to provide inspirational choral music for many of his functions. Frank worked with Barbara Bush, Paul Harvey, George W. Bush, Jane Seymour, and many others to generate funds for the non-profit foundation, which now holds and manages a fund greater than $61 million dollars.

Frank's biography mentions his interests in restoring and preserving historically important buildings. Frank even convinced Freda and me that we, too, could renovate a portion of our residence.

This story of our half-century friendship with Frank McMeen is one single thread of the many relationships Frank has made.

Frank told me being a writer and composing books was never part of his dreams. But a life-threatening heart surgery, in which his heart would be stopped and he would be placed on life support, brought Frank to an introspection that left him emotionally drained.

He composed himself, walked into the hospital, survived the surgery, and spent a month in recovery as a guest of one of his foundation board members. When finally he could ascend his host's stairs to the second floor in one trip, Frank returned home. It was yet another month before Frank could consider life again to be normal.

As Frank grew stronger, story after story began to take shape in his mind. Frank posted them on social media one at a time. Frank's many influential friends, some of them university presidents, urged Frank to publish a book. The result was *Let Me Tell You A Story: Finding Hope in a Hopeless World*.

Frank never intended to write a second volume, but we have *It's All About a Story: Be Encouraged* and now his third volume, *Your Life Is a Story: God Loves Every Page of Your Life*.

Frank is already thinking about Volume IV: *Stories from Along the Way: How Life Gives Us Lessons*.

Without reservation, I recommend this book. The chapter Frank most wants to be read and considered is Chapter One: "Rules and Regulations." Perhaps because of my advancing age, I recommend Chapter Fourteen: "How Shall I Be Remembered?"

Regardless, each chapter demands reflection, soul searching, and contemplation of eternity.

—John Robert Hall, founding conductor, A Cappella Singers, Freed-Hardeman University

Table of Contents

Acknowledgments — XV

Chapter 1: Religion and Rules — 1

Chapter 2: Troubled Times — 11

Chapter 3: Waiting — 15

Chapter 4: Thoughts on Psalm 11 — 21

Chapter 5: I Was This Skinny Kid — 25

Chapter 6: The Christmas Gift — 35

Chapter 7: Eyes Have Not Seen — 45

Chapter 8: Going on a Trip — 51

Chapter 9: Jonas Salk Saved the World — 57

Chapter 10: Biltmore Mansion — 69

Chapter 11: People — 75

Chapter 12: The Ties That Bind — 81

Chapter 13: Her Name Was Lucky — 89

Chapter 14: How Shall I Be Remembered? — 99

Chapter 15: Whoever, Wherever, Whatever — 105

About the Author — 111

Acknowledgments

This is book three.

By the time this book is published, I will have retired from a most wonderful job as president of the Community Foundation of West Tennessee. My forty-six-year career in the nonprofit world has provided me with the most amazing opportunities. Where else could I have gotten the chance to work with some of the most influential people of our time?

Art Linkletter, Paul Harvey, Jane Seymour, Gary Morris, Vince Gill, Amy Grant, Darryl Worley, Tom Landry, Mary Lou Retton, Senator and Ambassador Howard Baker, weatherman Willard Scott, Barbara Bush, news reporter Sam Donaldson, Vice President Dan Quayle, Brenda Lee, and record producer Norbert Putnam have touched my life. My brief glimpse into their lives affected me. Sometimes funny and mostly educational, these individuals made me a better person when I had the opportunity to spend a day or more with them.

Others such as Dr. Milton Sewell, Dr. Vicki Lake, John R. Hall, Libby Murphy, Dr. E. Claude Gardner, Dr. Lee Sheppard, Dr. Barnett Scott, Bobby Walden, David Shannon, and Dr. Billy Smith are not in that "famous" category, but they have played a critical role in my life and others.

My life has been, to many, a charmed life. I have found out that a "charmed life" tends to take a lot of work, determination, and commitment.

Clarence from *It's a Wonderful Life* was correct: "No man is a failure who has friends." I have truly been blessed by my friends. I hope this book blesses you.

"The Son of Man came to seek and to save the lost."

—Luke 19:10 (NIV)

CHAPTER ONE

Religion and Rules

There was a time in my life when I would have been a good Pharisee.

I was a rule-keeper. I didn't care about the outcome, because the rules were most important.

I followed lots of rules, including some from the Old Testament that we don't follow anymore—like not eating pork or shellfish, not wearing mixed fabrics, not touching dead things. We even had rules that we put in place to protect us from breaking the previous rules.

What does that even mean? Well, it means that I had become a Pharisee, because rules meant everything.

Without grace, rules are hard to live by. Rules became so important in the Christian community that churches divided over them or, in some cases, elevated them above the message. Church attendance was required. You were not allowed to miss even

Wednesday nights unless you were "providentially hindered." I guess that meant "unless God prevented you from getting to worship."

I've heard of churches that made rules to keep us from violating God's rules. We didn't have kitchens in our church buildings. We didn't want to risk violating Paul's suggestion, "Do you not have homes to eat in? Or do you despise the church of God?" As strange as it sounds, some church buildings didn't even have water fountains.

I was raised a good Pharisee. I was trained to keep rules.

Then I encountered Jesus.

What? Didn't Jesus follow the rules?

As a Pharisee, I would say that Jesus was a rule-breaker.

It took me a while to see the point that Jesus was making with three stories, three simple stories, in which Jesus emphasized what God wanted versus what Pharisees thought God wanted.

There was this one occasion when Jesus was in the area of Perea, headed to Jerusalem. This was near the end of His ministry, when He was going from town to town teaching.

Where Jesus taught, people gathered to listen. As usual, the crowd was pressing against Him and following Him to hear more. Everyone was enjoying the message except for one group: the Pharisees. The Pharisees saw a major problem in those who gathered to listen to Him. Jesus was encouraging tax collectors and sinners to come hear Him speak.

How dare Jesus speak and associate with those sinners? The Pharisees were so disturbed by what was happening that they started this whisper campaign against Jesus. He can't be from God, because He was associating with those ungodly people, the tax collectors and sinners.

That's a good thing, right . . . teaching sinners? Evidently not to Pharisees. You were not to associate with sinners. You were not to eat with them. You were not to have any fellowship with them.

Knowing this whisper campaign was going on behind the scenes, Jesus told three parables to the sinners and tax collectors so that the

Pharisees would hear. The stories were really addressed to them.

"Suppose you have a hundred sheep and lose one . . ."

"Suppose a woman has ten silver coins and loses one . . ."

"There was a man who had two sons . . ."

We know these stories. We probably learned them early in life.

The man who lost one of his sheep went out and found it. The woman who lost one of the ten coins lit every candle and lamp in the house, then swept the house clean until she found the lost coin.

Then Jesus tells the story of the lost son. We have strong feelings about this story.

We have emotional connections to the stories of the lost sheep and the lost coin. We can begin to relate to a lost son. Reading that story, our heart aches for the father. We connect with the story.

The story of the prodigal son is one of the most beloved stories in all sacred writings for a reason. The story worked on the tax collectors and sinners who heard it, but not on the Pharisees for whom it was intended. They missed the point completely.

Then there was the time when Jesus was traveling through Jericho. That day, as most days with Jesus, there was a massive crowd of people wanting to see and hear Him. Zacchaeus, the tax collector, a small man, was one of those in this large group.

Get lost in the crowd, or get ahead of the crowd? Well, Zacchaeus decided to run ahead of the crowd and climb up into a sycamore tree. He had the perfect spot to see Jesus as He came that way. Jesus continued walking and talking.

Jesus not only came near Zacchaeus, Jesus walked under the very tree where Zacchaeus was perched. He looked up, then called Zacchaeus out by name and in front of everyone there.

That day, there were probably so many people who would have loved it if Jesus had called them out by name. Even Pharisees seemed to have loved the notoriety of this famous person calling them out by name, but no one expected Jesus to call out Zacchaeus, a sinner . . . and Lord help him . . . a tax collector!

That day Jesus went home with Zacchaeus, a tax collector.

Dinner that night was probably way over the top. Zacchaeus was a wealthy man. Jesus was a famous teacher. I would assume that Zacchaeus provided a grand meal and invited all his wealthy and hated friends, who didn't meet the kosher status that the Pharisees demanded.

How dare Jesus go have dinner with such people?

What was going on in the mind of Jesus?

Would Jesus allow Himself to be entertained by such sinners? That dinner was probably not acceptable to any respectable Jewish person. Why in the world would Jesus do such a forbidden thing?

Jesus enjoyed a wonderful meal. He probably talked like most dinner guests would.

"Tell me about your family."

"What does a tax collector do all day long?"

"Where are your children in school?"

"Have you ever been to Rome?"

"What can I do to save on my taxes?"

"How about those Damascus Broncos? Do you think they will make it to the playoffs?"

I'm sure Jesus had typical conversations, until He wanted to talk to them about the real purpose of His visit.

I can imagine it now: Jesus standing up, tapping a few times on His water glass . . . uhhhh . . . maybe clay mug.

"Can I have your attention, please? What wonderful hosts you have been. I want to share something from my heart."

Then Jesus began telling about the love of God and the expectations of God.

Whatever the message was, it worked in a powerful way. The message worked so powerfully that Zacchaeus stood up and spoke freely.

"Lord . . ."

The room got quiet.

"Lord, I get it. I will be better! I will be a better neighbor, a better dad, and I will be a . . . a better child of God. Jesus, I am committing today to give half of my possessions away to help the poor, and if I have cheated anyone, I will repay them four times what I cheated them."

That night two messages were told. Jesus shared His eternal message that fell on the hearts of people looking for God, and Zacchaeus told the group that God had been working on his heart.

That night, in a room full of open hearts, Jesus announced to the group, and probably to a few Pharisees listening outside the door: "Today salvation has come to this house!"

What's that? Salvation?

Yeah, that's what Jesus said.

Salvation to the tax collectors?

Well, yeah, that is what Jesus said.

What? Salvation has come to the tax collectors and sinners even when the Pharisees condemned them and Jesus for even associating with them? Really?

Yeah, that's what happened. It was a powerful message!

What should we take away from these stories?

The Pharisees believed the opposite of what Jesus taught. To the Pharisees, you had to Behave and Believe, and then they would let you Belong.

You had to Behave: Do as I say. Stay kosher. Keep the rules.

You had to Believe: Follow all the rules we have in place.

All of that came before you could Belong: Be accepted into the fold.

Behave, Believe, Belong . . . in that order.

Jesus did not accept that.

To get His message across to the Pharisees, Jesus told the three stories: the lost sheep, the lost coin, and the prodigal son. The last story was the most extreme and unkosher.

"And when he came to himself, the prodigal son said, 'I will return to my father's house and be as a hired servant, because I am not worthy . . .' "

When the son reached a low point, the father reached a high point.

"The father saw him far away, walking that long road, and ran."

The father ran . . .

"Dad, I'm not worthy to be a son for what I have done," the son said.

The father yelled to the servants: "Get the best shoes and the best robe. Kill the fatted calf." And they began to celebrate. "My son who was dead is now alive. My son who was lost is now found."

Jesus told these stories not for the sinners and not for the tax collectors. Jesus told these stories to the Pharisees who viewed God as some heartless taskmaster. Jesus told these stories to the Pharisees who expected every debt to be paid and every injustice to be resolved.

We see in these stories an image of God that is different from what we have been taught and from what the Pharisees believed in.

I had always thought that God was up in Heaven mad at those of us on Earth because we sinned. If you died and had some unforgiven sin, God would send you to hell.

There were times as a child and a teenager that I felt that I was going to hell. I went to church on Sundays and Wednesdays, but if I had one sin for which I had not asked God's forgiveness, I would go to hell. I felt that God was mad at me, angry, frustrated. I was living my life struggling to be acceptable to God.

In 1741, Jonathan Edwards's fiery sermon, "Sinners in the Hands of an Angry God," imprinted vivid, terrifying imagery of hell and divine wrath on sinners during the First Great Awakening. That's how I thought God was. Religion was very legalistic. God was retributive and punished mankind for each sin. God was perfect, and if we were not perfect and failed to live up to His expectations, God sent you to hell.

You could go to hell for missing church. You could go to hell by "omission" . . . by not doing what God had said to do. My image of God was one that instilled fear.

These stories presented a completely different image of God.

From Scripture, we know that God is immutable. God does not mutate. God does not change. I always thought that meant that He was always angry and made it difficult to go to Heaven.

I now know that the fact that God does not change—God is immutable—means that the God that Jesus taught in these stories was the same God throughout the Old Testament.

We often fail to comprehend that we now know who God is. Through Jesus, and the stories of Jesus in the Gospels, we get a clearer picture of God.

Through Scripture, we see that "No one has ever seen God but the one and only Son, who has made Him known."

What? We can learn and see God through Jesus?

Scripture says that Jesus is the exact representation of God, not what we thought we saw through the Old Testament.

If we want to see God, we look at Jesus. If we want to see the nature of God, we look at Jesus.

Is God loving? Vindictive? Angry?

We see God through the life of Jesus. Jesus perfectly portrays God in His life and teachings.

I have heard this belief expressed this way, which makes it so clear: God is like Jesus. God has always been like Jesus. There has never been a time when God was not like Jesus.

We haven't always known that, but now we do.

The writer of the book of Hebrews stated, "Jesus is the exact representation of God's very being."

With Jesus being God, being sent from God, God treats people the very same way that Jesus treated people.

The story of the prodigal son shows us God.

We see His love for us sinners, bad sinners, dirty sinners, horrible sinners.

God and Jesus hold completely opposite positions from the Pharisees and many Christians today.

We talk today about whom God hates.

We talk today about who is not welcome.

We talk today about how dirty some sinners are.

Jesus, being God in the flesh, shared how God treats sinners.

Jesus got up in the midst of the sinners and tax collectors and talked to them, ate with them, loved them.

Jesus taught a new world order: Belong, Believe, then Behave.

Belong. I accept you. You belong WITH God's people. I will eat with you, associate with you, and enjoy company with you.

The Pharisees, then and now, do not allow such.

Believe. Jesus had this unique view of people. You don't throw rocks at people you are trying to convert. How interesting that we are so like Pharisees: "Condemn them to hell and try to scare them into being better."

How did that work for the Pharisees? It didn't.

How has it worked today? What good has come from expressing hate and condemnation? Hate breeds hate. Anger brings about more anger.

Belong. Believe. Behave.

Behaving is hard. We behave better the more that we belong and believe.

Once you take in the concept that God really, really, really loves you, your life begins to change.

Once you take in the concept that people really, really, really want you in their group and their lives, people behave.

The tax collectors and sinners changed once they were around Jesus. Everyone's life changed once they were around Jesus.

People who felt like they didn't belong had their lives changed by being around Jesus. People who didn't believe had their lives changed once they were around Jesus. People began to behave once they had been around Jesus.

The point? Whom do we exclude from Jesus? Whom do we not welcome to our churches?

With the prodigal son, the change didn't happen in the long walk home. It happened when the father let the son know this: Despite what you have done, despite where you have been, despite who you think you are, you still belong in this family.

How about you? Do you think God is angry?

Is He vindictive? Is He about to zap you?

Do you think He has rules that make Him send you to hell?

We learn about God in how Jesus interacted with the common man . . . sinners, tax collectors . . . people like you and me.

Did you ever find Jesus angry with the common man?

He fed them, cried over them because they were like sheep without a shepherd, ate with them, and cried over their graves.

Did Jesus ever act vindictive toward humanity?

We find Jesus in the midst of humanity. He didn't want to stone the woman caught in adultery as the Law of Moses required. He didn't even punish the Samaritan woman who had a long list of husbands and who was living with a man who was not her husband.

Even when they had Jesus arrested and tortured, He responded on the cross: "Father, forgive them, for they know not what they do."

When I picture God the Father, I am encouraged. God is like Jesus. Even when I see the difficult passages in the Old Testament, I must remember: God has always been like Jesus.

There has never been a time when God was not like Jesus.

God loves you just like the prodigal son's father loved him. The father was not vindictive or angry or requiring retribution for all the funds the son misused. The father simply wanted to restore the relationship. Forget the rules, I want my son, whom I love, back with me. I want him to BELONG.

Allow those we don't accept . . . or love . . . or like . . . to be around Jesus.

Thanks be to God for this unspeakable gift.

*"I saw the Lord sitting on a throne,
high and lifted up,
and the train of His robe filled the temple."*

—Isaiah 6:1

CHAPTER TWO

Troubled Times

Society is changing, and you may not feel safe. When the nation lacks leadership, what do you do?

What can you do? You have no real power.

Well, King Uzziah was sixty-eight years old when he died.

Uzziah had ruled the country for fifty-two years.

Imagine having a ruler who was good—very good—and on top of that, he was loved by his people!

He was the only leader that some of Israel had known. King Uzziah was a godly man and ruled Israel well. His death left a void.

When the people heard of his death, they were troubled—perhaps even worried.

"What will we do? Who will be our leader now?"

Some remember when John F. Kennedy was shot in Dallas. I do. People cried. The nation shut down for days.

"What will happen now that he has been killed?" "Who killed him?" "What kind of leader will we have next?"

The people of Israel had those same feelings. They loved Uzziah. They trusted him.

Isaiah gives us a picture of what was happening when King Uzziah died . . .

"I saw the Lord sitting on a throne, high and lifted up, and the train of His robe filled the temple." Seraphim flew and cried out, "Holy, Holy, Holy."

What? I don't get it. What does this have to do with unrest and leadership?

God wanted Isaiah to know something during this time of great national loss and social unrest, this time of questions and a void in leadership.

God is still in control. We are still His people. Governments are still in place by His choosing.

So, so many things in our world are upside down right now!

Maybe God is allowing this moment to teach us something.

But with all this unrest, people doubt. They tell themselves there are truths they need to know.

God is in control. We are His people.

God does not waver, even when there is social unrest. God's love for us remains sure! His character never changes. Nor should ours.

May you still find comfort and peace when our world is not at peace.

"*The Lord said to Abraham,
'Why did Sarah laugh and say,
'Will I really have a child, now that I am old?'
Is anything too hard for the Lord?
I will return to you at the appointed time
next year, and Sarah will have a son.'* "

—Genesis 18:13-14

CHAPTER THREE

Waiting

I hate waiting. Waiting usually involves lines. Long waits and long lines. Are you ever put on hold when you are calling some national/international company? Does your blood pressure go up and your temper become shorter?

I want to think that it was not always like this. My grandfather never talked about waiting in lines. My dad doesn't really complain. I never remember him complaining about being put on hold or waiting in line.

Evidently, times were different in previous generations. Laid-back. Slower-paced. Things I know little about.

During a recent trip to Egypt, I saw something that has not changed in thousands of years: Bedouins living in the desert.

I had dinner with some Bedouins the night before climbing Mount Sinai. The food was cooked traditionally over an open fire.

Bedouins have remained basically unchanged since biblical times.

Bedouins live in the desert areas of the Holy Land. They may not always live in tents, but they do live away from civilization and basically govern themselves as tribes. They herd goats or other animals in a seemingly laid-back lifestyle.

Long ago, Abraham was sitting under the canopy of his tent. He was enjoying the beauty of a sun-filled day in the Holy Land, with blue sky, the yellow of the terrain, the smell of goats.

Sitting and enjoying a quiet day, Abraham noticed three people far off approaching his settlement. Abraham did what Bedouins do. He approached them and invited them to come and stay for dinner.

It did not take Abraham long to realize that he was having an encounter with God.

The God Abraham worshiped, the God Abraham followed, is the God who revealed His will and made promises to Abraham.

Sometimes God's promises don't seem normal. Sometimes God's promises don't seem practical.

On that day, God made a promise. God made a promise so unusual that Sarah thought it was impractical—and funny. Sarah thought it was so odd that she laughed. Then she lied!

Sarah lied about laughing.

What God had said, what God had promised, what God was doing, was confusing.

"A year from now when I return, Sarah will have a child," God said.

Sarah was old. Abraham was old. Old people don't have children.

Getting pregnant when you are very old would be miraculous. That's not how our world works, not with miracles.

That's not how God works around here, Sarah thought.

You know, Abraham spent most of his life waiting. He had heard but didn't seem to fully believe it. He had heard that his small tribe would become a great nation. Abraham was going to bring forth the salvation of mankind.

What? We are just like Abraham and Sarah.

We try not to wait. We hate waiting. We have technology that helps prevent us from waiting for anything.

Our food is delivered to us, even from McDonald's. Our purchases are made online without ever entering a store. We even speed up delivery to get things faster than a regular delivery. You can get that purchase as early as tomorrow.

There are people working on getting everything possible done without waiting.

The Bible doesn't have much good to say about being in a hurry. Refusing to wait seems to carry with it bad outcomes.

Abraham and Sarah had trouble waiting.

Sarah gave Abraham her servant Hagar to help speed up the promise of God. Oh, the issues that created.

Waiting always seemed to be a problem.

King Saul had trouble waiting on Samuel, who was on his way to light the coals for the sacrifice. Tired of waiting for him, Saul stepped up and made the sacrifice. Oh, that decision began the downfall of Saul being king.

The prodigal son had trouble waiting for his inheritance from his father. "Dad, I want my inheritance now!"

The pace of our world seems to be, "It's got to be better if we get it faster."

Ever noticed the pace of God? The pace of God is slow.

"Wait for the appointed time . . . wait for it, because it will surely come," is how the prophet Habakkuk worded it. Habakkuk added, "The just shall live by faith."

He didn't say the just shall live by haste, but by faith.

There is a difference in what the world says versus what God says.

World: "Be loud." God: "Be still."

World: "Be upset." God: "Be at rest."

World: "Demand it now." God: "Have patience."

World: "Wait for nothing." God: "Wait for God."

Life happens in the waiting. If you can't be happy in the waiting, you probably won't be happy in life.

In Jerusalem, there is a unique design to the steps going up to the gates of the city walls where people went up the Temple Mount to enter the temple. The steps are meant for visitors to walk up, not to run.

You'll have a deep step followed by two shallow steps. Then you'll have a deep step followed by three shallow steps. They force you to walk up to the temple.

The steps were designed to slow you down.

Understand this: Culture is wrong. Culture is rarely wholesome.

Remember kids eating Tide Pods?

Culture does not emphasize things that help us become better people. Culture does not emphasize things that help us achieve better lives.

Sabbath. Silence. Contemplation. Prayer.

Notice the Twenty-Third Psalm: "He makes me to lie down in green pastures. He leads me beside the still waters. He restores my soul."

Read that again. God makes me lie down.

Why would God do that?

The entire chapter is about resting . . . relaxing . . . restoring.

Are you stressed with trying to juggle family and work?

Are the holidays nearly too much to handle . . . trying to squeeze in your family, his/her family, church stuff, social stuff?

Are the kids and work removing the romance and creating a world you never wanted? Life can be difficult and painful, putting more on your plate than you ever wanted.

The prophet Isaiah says, "Those who wait on the Lord shall renew their strength."

Wherever you are in this life—whether facing struggles or seeking help—wait upon the Lord. Sit with Abraham, and let the Lord's promises come to you.

Psalm 11

In the Lord I take refuge.
How then can you say to me:
"Flee like a bird to your mountain.
For look, the wicked bend their bows;
they set their arrows against the strings
to shoot from the shadows
at the upright in heart.
When the foundations are being destroyed,
what can the righteous do?"

The Lord is in His holy temple;
the Lord is on His heavenly throne.
He observes everyone on Earth;
His eyes examine them.
The Lord examines the righteous,
but the wicked, those who love violence,
He hates with a passion.
On the wicked He will rain
fiery coals and burning sulfur;
a scorching wind will be their lot.

For the Lord is righteous,
He loves justice;
the upright will see His face.

CHAPTER FOUR

Thoughts on Psalm 11

We live in times where we have been immensely blessed. We live in times where we wonder about our future as a country and the future of our health.

The more things change, the more they stay the same.

I can read and understand facts about God from Psalm 11.

No matter what happens on Earth, the Lord is in His holy temple and no human, no earthly event, can remove Him from His place. And while His throne is in Heaven, God knows how you handle situations.

God allows men to be challenged so those men can choose to do good toward others. Because man is challenged to do good, do not forget that God doesn't look kindly on people who do wicked things.

God remembers those who love to do evil things and create

violence. Bad things will happen to bad people. God allows it to happen to them because that is their world.

Do not forget, no matter what happens to you or your friends or this country, the Lord will never change His character. God will always allow good people to be rewarded and bad to be punished.

You do bad things, you get bad results. You do good things, you get good results. You sow the wind, you reap the whirlwind.

God loves good deeds and those who do them.

Remember, only good people shall behold His face, so do good and love others.

*"All those gathered here will know
that it is not by sword or spear
that the Lord saves; for the battle is the Lord's,
and He will give all of you into our hands."*

—1 Samuel 17:47

CHAPTER FIVE

I Was This Skinny Kid

When I was in the fourth grade, there was this kid who wanted to fight. I was walking home from school. I didn't know this kid. He didn't look familiar, and he wasn't in my class.

Caught off guard like that, about six blocks from school and probably ten blocks from home, I didn't know what to do. He was bigger than me and was daring me to fight. I was smart enough to know that some part of my body would probably be hurting if we fought.

"You must have mixed me up with my brother," I told him, and I kept walking.

I got home. It was a while before my brother got there. He took the long way home. I wonder why.

I never understood fighting.

Remember when King David was a little boy tending sheep?

Eliab, David's oldest brother, was standing in a crowd of King Saul's soldiers. They were all afraid of Goliath.

Who wouldn't have been? Goliath was the subject of all their conversations. He was out in front of Saul's fighting soldiers threatening them.

David appeared at the battle site. His father had sent him to bring some food to his older brothers in Saul's army.

David worked his way into the crowd. This small, ruddy boy walked among the tall, trained fighters. He overheard the soldiers' conversations, how they were nervous about what to do with Goliath. Eliab heard David ask what a man would get if he killed Goliath. Eliab exploded.

"Why are you even here? Who is taking care of your tiny herd of sheep?" Eliab demanded of his little brother.

Ouch.

Brothers can have differences.

My brother and I had disagreements. I laugh about them now.

When we were around nine or ten years old, we shared a bedroom. On one occasion, we had an argument so bad that we took masking tape and divided the room in half! From the dresser drawers to the closet, the room was split down the middle. Unfortunately, my brother's half had the door in and out of the room.

While it did not require the United Nations to negotiate a peace treaty, we agreed that I could have access to the door. When we were probably six and seven years old, there was no peace treaty in the back seat of the car.

I want to think it was my brother causing problems—always my brother, because I totally behaved myself. Well, usually. Then there was this one occasion. Touching/poking was involved.

There is nothing like seeing your brother sitting in the car, unpoked. Sooo, knowing it ticked him off, I reached over and touched his elbow. It ticked him off. So he touched me, then I touched him, then suddenly, he punched me!

"Momma!!!! Make Mike quit hitting me!"

"Mike, are you hitting your brother?"

"Well, Momma, it's his fault. He poked me!"

"Frank, quit poking your brother!"

I'm sure my parents got tired of us touching and poking. It always ended in Mom or Dad having to intervene. Somebody got touched every time we went anywhere. That still makes me laugh today.

The dynamics in David's family were probably interesting. Eliab was Jesse's oldest child; David was the youngest.

Before this encounter with Eliab, the prophet Samuel visited the house of Jesse to anoint a new king to replace King Saul after God had rejected Saul as king.

Samuel saw the older brother, Eliab, coming to make a sacrifice and said, "Surely the Lord's anointed is before him." Evidently, Eliab was handsome, tall, and impressive.

Don't you hate it when you have to compete against people with great physiques, perfect hair, the nicest of clothes? When most people find themselves competing with "perfect people," they feel that they have already lost. We have all been there.

Once I was asked to judge one of the competitions for Miss Tennessee.

During a contest for one of the younger titles in the competition, there was a girl who had won a preliminary title and a scholarship in her hometown and was now competing for a larger title.

She was smart. She had personality. But during the interview portion, she mentioned something that broke my heart. This young lady shared what her father told her before coming to this state competition.

"Why are you competing? You won't win! You are too fat."

My heart sank as she told us.

How could a father tell a daughter, one who had enjoyed some success, that she couldn't win—especially because she was "too fat"?

I made sure that I found that dad. I wanted to see if he would even show up to support his daughter. He was there. Later that evening, during a break in the competition, I met him. I controlled my tongue when I was talking to him.

This intelligent teenager didn't win the title, but she won my heart!

When Eliab, Mr. Perfect, was not chosen, Samuel looked at all of Jesse's children. The prophet went through all the sons who were there.

Soon Samuel ran out of options to be the king of Israel, so he turned to Jesse. "Do you have any more children?"

"Well, I do have this young son. He is out herding sheep, but you don't want him."

Jesse sent for his son, David, to come to the house.

A ruddy kid who had been minding the sheep came walking up to his father. He was the smallest and youngest, the least likely and the least important in the family.

God told Samuel, "Arise! This is the new king of Israel!"

Interesting how God chooses the most unlikely to make the most major point.

Remember Elizabeth, the mother of John the Baptist?

Elizabeth was way beyond child-birthing age, but God needed an Elizabeth to convince Mary that she would bring the Messiah into the world. Elizabeth was a nobody, yet she played a powerful role.

Remember Moses? He wasn't a speaker. He didn't see himself as a national leader.

Time and time again, God chooses the less likely, the unrecognized, the smallest.

He used the common to do the extravagant.

You already know this, but a raindrop can help make a rainbow.

Resistance can create a body builder.

We know the story. The shepherd boy David walked up to

Saul's army and faced their greatest warrior. David killed Goliath.

The least likely thing happened, and it fostered courage. Eliab and his buddies—tall, strong Marine types—had not believed any Israelite could kill Goliath.

Well, David was the opposite of what they thought it would take to defeat the enemy. David was the most unlikely champion. David, the least likely.

David gave the Israelites courage.

When I was in high school, sometimes I didn't do my homework. I would ask a friend in my class, "Did you get your homework done?" "No. Did you?" "Good, because I didn't either."

I found strength in surrounding myself not with the "A" students but with the "C" students.

Saul's army was like a group of "C" students. They felt okay with not addressing Goliath's challenges.

Tiny David charged at Goliath with only a sling and a small, smooth stone. That stone was God-driven. It went right to Goliath's only vulnerable spot.

Saul could have killed Goliath. Eliab could have killed Goliath. You could have killed Goliath.

Notice how things changed when Goliath was face-down on the ground, dead. David took the slain giant's sword and cut off Goliath's head.

Again, Eliab could have done that. Saul could have done that. You could have done that.

David knew what others had forgotten. He tried to remind them.

The big, muscular, tall, well-trained soldiers did not comprehend what David was saying.

Seeing that Goliath was now dead . . .

The Philistines lost courage. The Philistines ran in fear.

The Israelites gained courage. The Israelites ran after the Philistines.

God used the least likely to impact a nation. David's faith changed the outcome of the battle.

Seeing the mistreatment of his fellow man, Martin Luther King Jr. responded like David's question to Saul: "Who is this uncircumcised Philistine that defies the living God?"

A simple, black preacher changed American history. A poor, black woman sitting on a bus in Montgomery changed how some people could travel in America. A determined woman fought hard so that women could cast their votes in an election.

Regular people changed the direction of our country.

When the Philistines saw David cut off Goliath's head, the Philistines fled.

When Saul's men saw David cut off Goliath's head, they finally found their strength to fight.

They heard David's words when he confronted the nine-foot-seven-inch Goliath: "You come to me with sword and shield, but I come to you in the name of the Lord."

With that, David ran toward Goliath, and with a stone, David brought down Israel's most powerful enemy.

If you are reading this, you are probably not the most powerful. You are probably not the strongest. You are probably not the smartest.

You don't have to be. It does not take the strongest or the smartest to impact the most.

The most powerful action in our world is a touch. Touching a heart creates courage and provides hope in a world with little heart, or hope, or courage.

Today, our world needs a ruddy young man. Out in a field. Doing his menial tasks each day.

In that field with the sheep, David didn't know that he was preparing himself for a future time.

A time when leadership was lacking. A time when David's country needed him. A time when his fellow men had lost hope.

A time when even friends and family failed to see his strengths.

There was something special about the commonness of David. He learned it in the field and was tested in the field.

He told what he learned in the field to King Saul. "The battle is the Lord's."

Saul didn't listen.

He told what he learned in the field to Goliath. "The battle is the Lord's."

Goliath didn't believe him.

Many years later, David would write in the Book of Psalms, "the battle is the Lord's."

I remember one Sunday afternoon, when I was sitting under a tree on our family farm, Mom and Dad were sitting in the bench swing that hung down from one of the tree's large limbs.

It was a lazy, warm Sunday, and we were sitting there with sweet tea in hand.

By this time in life, my parents had grown to become my friends. Amazing how that transition happens. It caught me by surprise. Suddenly, conversations with Mom or Dad made sense. I used to not be interested in their opinions. Now I sought them.

So I was enjoying a simple Sunday afternoon with them, when Mom spoke up. It was not unusual for Mom to speak up. She always had a motherly opinion.

"We are very proud of you and Mike," she started.

Evidently, Mom and Dad had been talking about my brother and me. This made me wonder what had prompted that discussion between them.

"We wanted you to know . . ."

Oh, no. Mom and Dad had a deep conversation about my brother and me and felt the need to share it with me.

"We wanted you to know that there is nothing you can do that would make us ever stop loving you."

This was a lot deeper than I expected on a Sunday afternoon.

I had to work hard to hold off tears. That one statement gave me hope and courage to take on bigger-than-life challenges. I always kind of knew that was true, but when Mom said this, her belief in me became real.

Perhaps Jehoshaphat remembered the story of David when he was in trouble with the enemies of Judah, God's people.

They were in deep trouble. They might lose in battle.

He looked for an answer. He needed an answer.

He hoped that God's people would survive against the strongest people in the land. God gave him a much more powerful answer.

Jehoshaphat gathered all of Israel together—soldiers, women, children—and the Lord spoke. God's message was clear: "The battle is not yours, but the Lord's. You will do nothing to defeat this enemy."

To their surprise, the most unbelievable thing had happened. The enemies had fought and killed themselves.

Jehoshaphat and his men simply walked onto the battlefield with the enemies lying at his feet.

Our world is one of discord. Our world is one of division. Our world is one of dysfunction.

God has you in a field tending sheep. You may think that tending sheep is beneath you. Tending sheep is not a bad thing.

When it is time for you to rise to the occasion, be ready. God plans on using you when you expect His call the least.

Forty years of living in the land of Midian prepared Moses to lead God's people.

David tended sheep for years.

Joseph survived years after being sold into slavery for God to use him.

There will be dysfunction, discord, and division.

Conflict didn't distract David. He knew the battle was not his, and whoever leads the battle will win. Conflict didn't distract Moses. It didn't distract Joseph.

David could never have been anointed king if he had not spent time in the fields.

Look at where you are—leading a life that may seem so ordinary, so boring, so uneventful. That's where God is developing your strengths for when God needs you most.

Please know, God does not forsake His children. The fight for good is not about us.

The battle is the Lord's. God always uses the common to show His extravagance . . . while you are in the field.

"The heavens declare the glory of God, and the firmament shows us His handiwork."

—Psalm 19:1

CHAPTER SIX

The Christmas Gift

It was a typical Christmas with my family. We were at my grandparents' home as was our custom. This year's Christmas turned out to be one of the most eventful Christmases of my life.

I was in the middle of my junior year in high school—a typical school year but an unbelievable Christmas.

We had a great meal with turkey and dressing and all the fixings cooked entirely by my grandmother. It was delicious!

Then came the designated time for opening presents. This was kind of a formal affair. My grandparents rarely let us kids into the living room.

Everything about that room had been the same since the house was built. The same couch, chairs, lamps, tables. You only went into the living room on special occasions, typically Christmas and Thanksgiving.

I counted the occasions. By the time I was seventeen years old, I had only been in that room about thirty-four times!

Whoever was Santa that year, usually Uncle Bill, would pass out beautifully wrapped presents to family members one at a time.

The rules were strict. One person at a time would open a gift and show it to everyone in the room. Everyone would "ooooh" and "ahhhh" as the official unwrapping of presents continued.

Mike and I were the only grandchildren present each Christmas. There were other grandchildren, but their belief system didn't allow for the exchange of Christmas gifts. I didn't understand it then and don't really understand their viewpoint even now, so we enjoyed being the only grands who were there.

When you were in elementary school, you received gifts from everyone. As I grew up, grandparents and aunts began to move us into the status level of getting socks, shirts, and ties for Christmas.

As teenagers, Mike and I were as tall or taller than any other family member. That meant we were getting adult Christmas presents.

The gift of white socks induced the "oooohs" and "ahhhhs" from everyone and eye rolls from us.

On one occasion, seventy-year-old Uncle Bill gave us ties that he liked. We proudly held up unique ties for everyone to see. We thought we might be the only kids in the ninth grade who received ties, but then again, we were probably typical.

I wore that tie to church only the next Sunday, so that my grandmother would tell my great-aunt Articeil and great-uncle Bill, who lived in Nashville, how nice it looked when she reported back that I wore it. Bill and Articeil, who had no children, were happy that I wore the tie.

When I was a junior in high school, Christmas was basically about parents exchanging gifts with grownups. We were no longer cute little kids. For a couple of years, we were viewed as adults and destined to receive ties, socks, and shirts.

On Christmas, as the day wound down, people would begin to gather their gifts, and Mike and I would help them carry everything to their cars.

One year, something quickly changed.

This one Christmas—a Christmas of shirts, ties, and socks—became the most amazing Christmas.

Everyone had loaded all the presents into their cars. The wrapping paper was off the floor, and the food was back in the refrigerator. The living room had again become the hallowed place you didn't enter except for special occasions: Christmas and Thanksgiving.

Then something unusual happened. My mother asked me to come into the living room/dining room. This was kind of strange.

For Mom and Dad to bring me back and for me to find Articeil and Bill standing alone in this room was odd. I thought that Nannie, my grandmother, had shut down this room for kids for the season. It was expected to open again only when Thanksgiving came around.

There they stood, waiting on me. I had never had much of a conversation with them other than telling them that I liked the socks they gave me.

"Frank, Articeil and Bill have something to give you."

Aunt Articeil handed me an envelope. On the front was written: "If Frank goes to Europe." Inside there was a lot of money—big bills, thousands of dollars, enough money for a high school junior to spend an entire summer as an exchange student on the other side of the ocean.

I was at the awkward stage of not knowing how to respond to situations like that.

I stuttered, "Thank you," but that seemed inadequate. I was a teenager, so hugs were not a big thing or a cool thing, but they were totally needed on this occasion.

Aunt Articeil and Uncle Bill hugged me and said, "We want

you to be able to go to Europe as an exchange student."

It was quite an honor to be considered as an exchange student, to live with families across Great Britain, Europe, and Russia.

Our family couldn't afford that trip.

This trip meant living overseas for the three months of summer. It meant living with families who were not your typical Tennessee families but allowed students to spend the summer learning about different cultures. I had written off being an exchange student because of the expense.

What do you do when someone does something far greater than you expected or could imagine?

Articeil and Bill gave me a summer that was amazing and life-changing. So many unique opportunities were now available.

Who do you know who was able to go behind the Iron Curtain? What would it be like to live with a family in the Alps of Austria?

Who do you know is able to live for weeks in Ukraine and learn that it was the breadbasket of the Russian world of its day? Or learn to eat with your fork in your left hand in the Netherlands?

Who do you know who would be able to live for weeks in Moscow and notice that, for a world power, they were living as America had a generation earlier? Their cars were the style my grandparents knew in America in the 1940s.

I saw the Blue Danube and found out that it wasn't blue.

I attended a real joust—where men on horseback hit challengers with long poles to knock each other off the horses—inside the walls of the Tower of London.

After an amazing summer, perhaps the best part was the delight of our plane landing in New York City on American soil, where I knew I was safe from any type of totalitarian governmental control.

What an amazing gift from Articeil and Bill. It became an ongoing blessing throughout my life. I experienced what so many others were not able to experience.

I'm sure there were other families with a son or daughter like me. Like us, they could not afford sending a child to Europe as an exchange student.

Not everyone had an Articeil and Bill.

Those parents, like mine, probably left a school meeting about the opportunities but never found a way to fund such a trip. Disappointments and missed opportunities happen in high school. They happen in real life to adults.

Life is tough . . . hard . . . not fair.

Not every family can afford to buy a house. Some people can afford a car that is only hundreds of dollars, not tens of thousands of dollars.

Living in America can be tough; some see no hope of living how others live.

Living can be difficult. There's the fragility of life and the special gift of life.

Dealing with life when you lose a parent. Dealing with life when you lose a child. Dealing with life when you face a battle with death.

Being close to losing life, a parent, a child, or a spouse, you begin seeing your existence as a special gift.

The Bible says we are given about three score and ten years: seventy years.

If we are given seventy years, that seems like an eternity to a ten-year-old. But to a spouse putting a loved one in hospice, life seems oh so short.

At the time of this writing, I have a dad who has lived, and lived well, for more than ninety years. Due to a farm accident, I began to see the fragility of life. Dad, who was probably going to live past one hundred years, was placed in hospice care.

Life is such a gift, the value of which becomes apparent at the end. We bring life into the world.

As far back as when God said, "Let there be light."

Of His own choosing, of His own will, God began the process of bringing you into this world. For one reason.

"Let there be a sun."

"Let there be a moon."

One star we call the sun, one solar system, and one green planet are all for one reason, a single reason . . .

God loves you. Follow me here.

"The heavens declare the glory of God and the firmament shows us His handiwork."

Why was all of that created?

It was created for you to see Him and His glorious nature. God is trying to get a message across to you.

God has placed millions of gifts before us: stars, planets, mountains, and rainbows, to name a few.

The complexity of an eye . . . the elegance of massive, two-hundred-year-old trees . . . the glorious nature of a waterfall . . . and the simple beauty of a bluebird.

They are all gifts. Gifts to you, to show you His glorious nature.

I know what some are thinking . . .

"No, Frank, you're wrong. We are part of this massive cosmos by luck. You see, there was a big bang, things flew out, a watery mess evolved into a living being, basically a fish that eventually became more refined and developed unique features to live on land. Over time, that thing became man."

Hogwash!

You . . . as you read this . . . you were placed into a wonderful and beautiful world because God loves you and wants you to see His glorious majesty.

Again, do not stop reading.

This world was made FOR YOU, because He loves you. You are here, and all around you is a gift, a gift from the Creator who loves you more than anything on this small, green planet.

This life is not a game, and he who gets the most wins. Life is not a competition where some will be winners, and some will be losers. If that is your concept of life, you were told a horrible lie.

Let's pretend for a minute. Let's say you now possess everything that this earth holds.

Then what?

If you gain all the treasures of this world, it's all yours. What do you win?

Every palace is yours; every bank is yours. You have so much money that you cannot even comprehend it.

What do you do after that?

Life becomes boring.

I have a college friend who is a physician. He was from a typical family who worked hard. They sent him to college, where he succeeded as a student. His hard work got him accepted into medical school. He graduated and joined the military as a physician. His work paid off his medical school loans.

After a couple of decades of working as a physician, he had all his bills paid and sent his kids to a Christian school and then a Christian college with no loans.

Sitting on a great bank account, with a successful career and successful kids, he asked me to have coffee with him. We talked for a long time.

What do you do when everything you've done has been successful with hard work? What do you do when you make so much money that it seems unreal?

"Frank, my life has no meaning," he told me over coffee. "I want to do something that impacts life."

"Everything you do at work impacts life. Your teaching at church is impactful," I pointed out. "What do you mean?"

"I want to give it all up and teach school," he told me.

This confession, this dream, came from someone who "gained the whole world" and found little solace in it.

What if you gain everything that this world holds and face

terminal cancer? What then? What if you lose the love of your life? What then?

There is only one reason that you were given life, and it was not to win everything.

You were given life so that God can show you that He loves you.

That's it. The stars are for you. The beautiful evening moon is for you.

God created everything in this beautiful world as a gift to the most precious of all creation: you.

Why would God love you? Why would the Creator love you so much? Because love is God's nature. Love is what He is.

God is love, and God's nature has always been love.

God created an amazing place so that you can see Him and His majesty and that He loves you.

We misread Scripture at times to fit into our Western culture.

"The wages of sin is death." Often we stop there.

We seem to miss the extravagance of the next phrase ". . . but the FREE GIFT of God is eternal life."

What? Immortality, starting now. It's a gift to you.

Jesus told His disciples, "I go away but will come and get you, so that where I am, there you may be with me."

Not trying to be too sappy here, but Jesus came for one reason, and that reason is YOU.

He came to give you life . . . immortality. We learn that through the life of Jesus.

I heard a preacher say something that stuck in my mind. In Jesus, Scripture gives us a picture of God that we had not seen before.

God is like Jesus. God has always been like Jesus. There has never been a time when God was not like Jesus. The more I study, the more I see the truth in this.

God is LOVE. God loves you.

Be blessed in that knowledge and show His love.

*"What eyes have not seen,
what ears have not heard,
what the heart cannot imagine,
is what God has prepared
for us who love Him."*

—1 Corinthians 2:9

CHAPTER SEVEN

Eyes Have Not Seen

Our villa was on a high cliff overlooking the ocean outside the beautiful hamlet of Port Maria, Jamaica.

This was the perfect place to watch a beautiful Jamaican sunset. We loved coming in from a long day in the small city and sitting on the cliff to watch the sun set.

It was not unusual to sit on the ledge at night and see storms on the horizon. We were so high over the beach below that you couldn't hear the waves splashing onto the sand. Nor could we hear the thunder from those large, faraway storms.

Still visible after sunset, there were high, classic thunderstorm clouds. Lightning lit them up beautifully, but it was a silent light show, a show so far out in the ocean that there was no sound.

The Jamaicans who were helping our church group get settled in didn't seem to notice the spectacular light show a few miles off the coast. To those working at our villa, the storm was an everyday sight. It happened in their neighborhood nearly every night.

Oh, what a sight!

On another trip, I went to an African village way back at a jumping-off place in Sierra Leone. The village was small but was the connecting point for hundreds of families living as they have done for hundreds of years.

We met with the chief and gained approval to treat sick children. Setting up our clinic didn't take too long. I had time to wander. I walked out from the center of the village to explore the surrounding area.

I found a path where villagers traveled daily. It was not a long walk before I saw the most amazing sight!

The area reminded me of old Tarzan movies. Rich, green tropical plants, with no sound other than my walking through the greenery.

The silence of nature was almost overwhelming as I walked up to the edge of a deep, verdant canyon, like the Grand Canyon, but everything was green with rainforest vegetation. There was a mist coming out of the deep green trees below.

I stopped and tried to take it all in. The sounds of nature were unfamiliar to me. I noticed that, amid the greenery at the canyon's bottom, smoke from a fire rose above the trees. Without a breeze, the smoke rose straight up, letting me know a family lived right around that fire in the middle of nowhere.

Oh, what a sight!

I stood amazed at the sight of that massive grand, green canyon.

To those who lived in the area, this huge ravine was just their neighborhood. This sight that amazed me was something that the people thought was commonplace. Just their neighborhood.

I think further back, to when I was an exchange student.

I was a high school junior staying with a wonderful family

in a small village in Austria. I met my host "mother and father." Picking up my big suitcase, we began the trip to the house from the airport. Their traditional Alpine home was on a curvy and isolated road, not near anything except their church and a store.

That evening, their son, my homestay brother, had planned a bonfire with his friends to welcome me into their family. Meeting so many Austrians my age was fun. We sat around the bonfire, and one of the guys began to play his guitar and sing.

I didn't know the songs, until they began singing, *"Take me home . . . country roads . . . to the place . . . I belong . . . West Virginia . . . Mountain Momma . . . take me home . . . country roads."*

They were so proud that they knew an American song. They had learned it so I could sing with them. I found out later that they had no idea where West Virginia was or who "Mountain Momma" was. I grinned.

As the sun was setting, I walked away from the bonfire and looked out at this huge mountain range of the Alps. What an amazing sight.

The edge of that flat area of the Alps was evidently a regular site for their many bonfires. I saw no roads, no cute Alpine homes. From that vantage point, I saw no sign of human beings. Majestic mountains seemed to disappear into the clouds.

Oh, what a sight.

No one came over to stare at the view with me. They saw it every day. It was just their neighborhood.

The beauty of this earth is breathtaking. I remember seeing the images from the Hubble Space Telescope!

Oh, the beauty of the heavens, more amazing than what our simple eyes can see. God created the majestic beauty of the heavens, visible only from a high-powered telescope.

Oh, what a sight!

Then I think of a Nashville friend tending to her dying mother, who told of amazing things she saw in her last few minutes of life.

From what the daughter told me . . .

Oh, what a sight!

"What eyes have not seen, what ears have not heard, what the heart cannot imagine, is what God has prepared for us who love Him."

A child describes what he saw when he left this world on a hospital emergency room gurney, with family gathered around.

"What eyes have not seen, what ears have not heard, what the heart cannot imagine, is what God has prepared for us who love Him."

Before COVID, we had a volunteer program called "No One Dies Alone" in Jackson where we would sit with patients who were dying and had no family.

Even though they could not respond, we played music. Even though they could not answer, we talked with them. Even though they could not pray along, we prayed over them.

I was amazed as I began to imagine what they might be seeing at that stage of the end of life.

"What eyes have not seen, what ears have not heard, what the heart cannot imagine, is what God has prepared for us who love Him."

It's scary to face death. There is fear for those who face death. There is a certainty that we all face death.

"What eyes have not seen, what ears have not heard, what the heart cannot imagine, is what God has prepared for us who love Him."

If I thought Jamaica had the most amazing sight . . . if I thought Austria had the most amazing sight . . . if I thought Africa had the most amazing sight . . . if I thought that the Hubble Space Telescope brought to view the most amazing sights . . .

I long to see what my mother saw. I long to see what my dad saw, as Dad was dealing with end-of-life issues in hospice.

Someday I will see it. Someday you will see it.

"What eyes have not seen, what ears have not heard, what the heart cannot imagine, is what God has prepared for us who love Him."

May the peace of God guard your hearts and minds.

"He will wipe every tear from their eyes. There will be no more death or mourning or crying or pain, for the old order of things has passed away."

—Revelation 21:4

CHAPTER EIGHT

Going on a Trip

We didn't go on many vacations as I grew up. Dad trained Tennessee Walking Horses, and we spent our summers going to horse shows on weekends and preparing for those shows during the week.

There was this one time that we had a real vacation. We were going to Florida!

Perhaps we were eight or nine years old. Dad was around thirty, with mom in her twenties. We prepared for weeks. This was before the internet. Mom called and made reservations for our stay. We were in a two-story hotel right on the beach. It was perfect!

My grandmother, Berf, made stuffed animals for us to play with on the trip. One of the owners of a horse in training let Dad borrow his station wagon so we could play in the back on the way to Florida. We loaded the car with pillows and blankets so my brother Mike and I could sleep most of the way down. We left at night so we could arrive early the next day. Driving while kids were asleep was probably so much easier.

It was daylight when we arrived. We were so excited to see the ocean for the first time!

There was a pool at the hotel, right outside our door. You could walk down to the beach just beyond the pool. We felt like we had died and gone to Heaven! Everything was perfect.

I don't know who enjoyed the trip more—Mom and Dad, because they got a relaxing week on the beach, or Mike and me, because our parents worked hard to make the trip so special for two excited boys.

A long, difficult trip with two young kids made perfect.

My friend Jenny took a trip to Nashville to be with her mom, who was in her last days of a horrible disease. Jenny went to spend each of those final weeks with her mom. Weeks dwindled to a few remaining days, and Jenny spent that time with her mom in a Nashville hospice house.

On Jenny's first or second day with her mom in hospice, her mom told Jenny about her visitors that day. There were many from church, many from her neighborhood. Each morning, Jenny would hear about more visitors who had been to visit.

Jenny's mom would list the guests. It was a typical morning ritual, name after name: Daniel and Sarah and Michael.

One morning, Jenny walked into the room and kissed her sweet mother. She showed her mom the flowers she'd brought and put them in the window.

Her mother was weak, but she wanted to talk. Jenny listened as she held her mom's hand.

"Oh, I must tell you about my visitors. There was Daniel . . . and Sarah . . . and Michael."

Jenny responded, "Oh, how nice of them that they keep coming back."

Jenny's mother smiled.

"Oh . . . and Michael," she said weakly, "he was not going to be able to be come back anymore. But they are all here."

Jenny looked around the room. No one was there. Jenny looked back at her mother, who was growing weaker.

Jenny's mother continued in her weak voice. "But they are all still here . . . don't you see them?"

Jenny broke down as she felt her mother pass from this life. She held her mother tightly as she experienced Heaven taking this precious child home.

Then there was Dad.

On September 14, at two o'clock in the morning, Dad began his departure.

Mom and Dad had been married sixty-five years. They were just kids when they met and married. Mom was too young to be married in Tennessee, so they went to Mississippi. Dad's brother, John, drove them to the big city of Iuka.

After being together for over six decades, September 14 began their reunion, this time for eternity.

This night became different.

Sometime around two o'clock on that Saturday, the room changed. I could tell that Dad was beginning his departure. The room was quiet.

Afterward, stepping outside, I could sense a stillness on the farm. All was calm, all was quiet.

That night, the den took on the invisible radiance of an unseen angelic presence. That night, a heavenly host arrived to heal an earthly problem.

That night, Dad was asleep in his recliner, in his den, but woke up in his true home where Mom was waiting.

A heavenly host escorted Dad into a place prepared for him.

Dad's last enemy—death—was overcome in victory. Dad faced his last trial, a trial that turned into a triumph.

Dad was at the bank of a historic river, the Jordan, crossing into the Promised Land. Mom and a heavenly host welcomed Dad into the holy city of Zion.

And so will we, as His children.

His heavenly hosts will escort us home, turning death into the most blessed fulfillment of the promise.

Beulah Land. Paradise. The Home of the Soul.

Our family longs for that grand reunion.

"Jesus answered, 'Everyone who drinks this water will be thirsty again, but whoever drinks the water I give them will never thirst. Indeed, the water I give them will become in them a spring of water welling up to eternal life.' "

—John 4:13-14

CHAPTER NINE

Jonas Salk Saved the World!

Polio destroyed millions of lives. Born in 1914, Jonas Salk began to work on polio vaccines as a medical student.

On March 26, 1953, Dr. Salk announced to the world on CBS that he had a vaccine that would wipe out the children's crippling disease called polio. His discovery began to change the lives and futures of children in 1954 when American children began to receive the vaccine.

I believe Dianne Odell was fifty-five years old when I met her for the first time. During her lifetime, Dianne was considered to be the oldest living iron-lung polio patient in the world. She had caught the disease before the vaccine was available.

Our first meeting was in her rural Madison County home, while her parents sat in the living room. I sat beside the iron lung and talked over the noise of the continually working bellows that allowed Dianne to breathe. To her, the sound was probably natural, as natural in her life as the sound of birds singing in a forest. That environment was the world in which she had grown up and in which she had lived for over fifty years by the time we met.

As the iron lung provided her breath to speak, I was amazed to find her highly intelligent and well-spoken for someone limited by a dreaded disease, living in an iron lung, and with limited access to the world.

What an amazing person, touching every life she encountered.

We talked of church, of our alma mater, and of hummingbirds.

Dianne loved church. She loved her college experience. The hummingbirds were continuously feeding off the sweet red juice in the feeders off the back porch during the summer months.

I thought that was an odd combination for someone having limited experience with any of those three.

Being in an iron lung meant Dianne rarely was able to be transported to church. Church was almost a day-long ordeal. Iron lungs are iron—a nine-foot-high, long iron tube. Kind of hard to transport. You had to take the iron lung with Dianne inside, with continuous electricity to keep the iron lung bellows pumping.

Dianne attended college on a scholarship, with an iron lung that limited her college experience. She lived in a professor's basement right off the campus, and Freed-Hardeman University brought the classes to her.

Again, the iron lung limited Dianne's ability to go outside her home to see the hummingbirds. That didn't stop her love for those amazing little birds.

Each of those topics was special to her. I think it is like tasting a sweet dessert for the first time; you want more of that wonderful experience.

She treasured each of those wonderful experiences and wanted to taste those experiences again and again, so on my first visit with her, we talked about those things.

When I left her room that day, I felt like a better person.

Dianne was so special. She had purity of mind, in that she had only seen the good in people—even good, caring, famous people.

Jane Seymour would travel from California to help raise money for Dianne's care. Gary Morris, singer and songwriter, would travel from Colorado to perform for her. So many famous people joined the rest of us trying to show Dianne that we cared. Everyone she encountered was kind to her, trying to make her life better.

Walking to my car after that first visit, I wondered: *Outside of Dianne's family and church friends, who cares about her?*

Dianne eventually spent nearly sixty years of her life in an iron lung, but who would care? She just lived in an iron lung. How in the world would she impact lives so that someone would care?

Why would someone care about your life when every minute is spent inside an iron lung? How could you provide anything impactful to our world?

I am sure that Dianne asked that very question a lot.

"Does my life really matter?" "Does anyone really care about me?" "Am I a burden on society?"

Dianne has not been the only person who has asked that question about his or her own life.

Driving away from her home, I began to reflect on so many people who get lost in society.

Many days on the way to work, I stop at McDonald's and get a large Diet Coke. There's the person who talks to me when I order at the drive-through. There's the person who collects my payment at the first window. There's the person who hands me my drink with a smile.

I have witnessed customers who were in the car in front of me being rude to these people in the service industry, perhaps feeling that they were beneath them. Perhaps the servers failed to get an order correct. Perhaps it took longer than expected. Customers felt that it was okay to be rude and unkind. Hardworking food service people, making minimum wage, are easy targets for anger.

Do these workers ever wonder if anyone they encounter really does care?

Every Tuesday and Friday, two gentlemen pull up to my neighbor's house in a pickup to get their garbage, and then one of them walks over to my house and gets my garbage and carries it to their truck to haul it away. They never complain and always exceed my expectations.

I wonder if it ever crosses their mind: Does anyone care about who I am and that I have a life beyond my job of picking up garbage?

I must confess that until this writing, I've never much thought about the garbage crew members and what they do, where they live, and how they deal with life. In the couple of years that I've lived in my home, these men come very early in the morning to pick up my garbage. I rarely see or hear them, but each week they show up and do their work.

I am probably quite typical in that I don't think about the many people I encounter. They are doing their job, and I am doing mine.

There have been times in my life when I wondered if anyone cares about me. Surely many others ask themselves that same question.

Sometimes people find themselves in a desert, questioning their importance.

Sometimes people find themselves facing a mountain, questioning, why climb it?

Sometimes they find themselves crossing a river, thinking they will drown. They find themselves alone, wondering if anyone cares.

Then there are times when people in our society do horrible acts to others, and we wonder why.

There are times when strangers take a weapon and shoot children in schools. Many children.

When these things happen, we wonder . . . why?

There has to be something that pushes them to the limit. Maybe in their minds, they believe that no really one cares about them. Something pushes people past the breaking point. Is it that they think that no one really cares about them, so why should they care? So they do horrible acts.

Does anyone care?

How many times a day do I encounter people who have asked themselves: "Does anything I do impact anyone?"

Does anyone really care about me?

Odd how we discount so many lives. Good people working in low-paying jobs go to work each day. Without them, many things we take for granted would not happen. Garbage collectors, fast-food workers, and convenience store employees are just a few of those who serve their customers.

I've never had my garbage man complain to me. Wait staff at restaurants have never complained to me. I've never had a convenience store worker pull me aside and talk about wanting a pay increase or better hours.

Walk in their shoes. Stand at that counter. Think as they might: I'm not a doctor who saves lives. I'm not negotiating national treaties that impact lives. I just work at McDonald's. No one cares about me or what I do. If I were to die tomorrow, it would not make a difference to anyone.

Think of the single mothers who get up each day, fix breakfast, get kids fed, get them dressed, get them on the school bus, then get dressed and go to work. They do all their morning mother stuff, then work all day, come home, do more mother stuff, and start it all over again the next day. Day after day after day after day, their life goes on, and they ask . . . "Does anyone care?"

All over this country, in every city, there are people who want to matter. All they want is to do something . . . *something* . . . so that someone cares.

It doesn't matter what kind of job they have.

The janitor who comes to your office and picks up your garbage—that man wants someone to care.

That teacher who struggles to reach disruptive students? All she wants is to do something, *something*, so that she can tell that someone cares.

The homeless man wasn't always homeless. He never could deal with the loss of his wife and child. After the funeral, he became lost, alone, empty. No one cared.

People search, hurt, struggle.

Life pushes people. Sometimes life pushes people to a point where it touches a nerve . . . a very important nerve.

We have all been close to that point but regained our composure. Some don't.

A spouse who has lost the dearest one after sixty-five years of marriage is left dealing with extreme loneliness.

Does Jesus care?

Living in a nursing home, a veteran struggles physically and mentally. He is over eighty years old but in his mind is still much younger. No one comes to visit, and he feels like a burden.

One time Jesus decided that He needed to go to Galilee.

There were two routes: One went around Samaria in the traditional Jewish way, and the other went through Samaria. Well, Jesus decided to walk through Samaria. Jews didn't do that. Samaria was forbidden territory. The Samaritans were people who decided not to marry a Jewish person. They married gentiles. That was a very bad sin back then, evidently. Jews would go out of their way not to travel through Samaria.

Why would Jesus travel through a forbidden country?

I'm sure Jesus was a good Jewish guy, keeping the Law, faithful in His attendance—you know, going to "church" and eating only the food that was "clean" and not working on the Sabbath.

This trip was different. That trip to Galilee was perhaps so that He *could* go through Samaria!

Jesus was on a mission, but He was tired on this day. Or He used that as an excuse.

"Hey, guys. Let's stop at Jacob's Well. I need some water and food. Why don't y'all go into the city and buy food? I'll sit here by the well and enjoy some water."

Perhaps this was planned.

He sat there in a forbidden country, according to Jews, and waited for the least likely of people: a Samaritan woman.

No, this was not an unplanned meeting—at least not for Jesus.

Jesus probably waited to leave Judea and planned for the right time, when He would arrive at Jacob's Well.

He wanted to arrive at the right time, so that He would meet a woman who probably had wondered if her life mattered. So He sat there, and right on time, she came to the well. Jesus spoke to her.

"Hey, can you give me a drink of water while you're getting yours?"

I don't know how she could tell, but this woman knew that Jesus was Jewish. Like He didn't know, she told Jesus that she was a Samaritan.

She knew this was unusual. She was perplexed that He even spoke to her.

"How is it that you, being a Jew, asked me for a drink of water? Jewish people do not talk to Samaritans."

Jesus told her . . .

"If you knew who it was asking you for a drink of water, you would ask Him for 'living water.'"

The woman didn't get it.

"What? You don't even have anything to draw water from this well, so how in the world can you give me 'living water'? Are you greater than our father, Jacob?"

"Everyone who comes here and drinks water from this well will be thirsty again," Jesus told her. "I will give them water that springs up into eternal life."

She still didn't get it.

"Sir, give me this 'living water' so that I don't have to keep coming to this well and drawing water," she said.

That day, the most interesting conversation took place between the Creator of the world and . . . a woman. A woman who had lost at love multiple times, who was not the most likely to feel good about her position in life. She was the most excluded—yes, excluded—from religion because of someone's marriage in her lineage. Remember, they married outside of the Jewish faith.

Perhaps Jesus's arrival was right on time, when she was at the does-anyone-care stage in her life, the perfect time for Jesus to enter the picture.

Jesus asked about her husband. She replied that she did not have a husband. Jesus took her statement one step further.

"You are correct in that you do not have a husband. In fact, you have had five husbands, and the person that you are living with is not your husband."

Ouch. Jesus got personal real quick.

She now knew something was different about Jesus. Excluded by the Jewish people, this Samaritan woman wanted to talk about religion.

Perhaps this is why Jesus decided that He needed to walk through Samaria by way of Jacob's Well. Perhaps this was why Jesus wanted to stop there and why He sent the disciples to go buy food. They didn't quite get everything Jesus was teaching and didn't need to spoil this moment.

Perhaps this is why Jesus had no cup, no jar for water, but waited for a woman to come and draw water. A certain woman.

This day at Jacob's Well became the perfect backdrop for a woman rejected by husbands and religious communities to talk about religion.

Jacob's Well was a religious icon for her.

She knew her spiritual lineage, even when religion had rejected her. Finally, there was something in which she could take pride.

This well, Jacob's Well, connected her to her faith, to her God, when she thought all had rejected her.

That day, this woman shared her faith with Jesus. She told Him their (hers and His) forefathers worshiped on the mountain there, but the Jews said that people should worship in Jerusalem. This Samaritan woman told Jesus she knew that God was going to send the Messiah.

That day, she shared her faith about the coming Messiah, the one she longed for and expected. She believed in this so much that she shared her faith, unknowingly, to the Messiah Himself.

That day became a day of confessions. Two astonishing confessions were made.

That day, she confessed her belief in the coming Messiah. And on that day, Jesus confessed to her—the most rejected person in the most rejected race, the woman excluded even from the most despised of people—that He was the Messiah.

When she heard that, confessions stopped, conversations stopped, but minds kept processing.

"What did He just tell me?" she must have asked herself. "What did I hear?"

Then a pot dropped, cracked, silence. Imagine how her reaction might have gone:

"Sir . . . uhhhh . . . I think I heard you say that you are the Messiah."

"I am the Messiah."

"You don't look like a Messiah. You look like me! You asked me for water. Messiahs don't ask people like me for water."

"I am the Messiah."

"Messiahs don't act like you. You talked to me. Important people don't talk to me. No one has ever talked to me like you have."

"I am the Messiah."

The seed was planted. She found herself face to face with the Messiah.

Interrupting this spiritual moment, the disciples returned to find Jesus with a Samaritan woman. It was quite unusual.

Everything got quiet again.

Jesus got quiet. The woman got quiet. The disciples got quiet.

Then the woman did the only thing she knew to do . . . run.

This woman ran to town and became a preacher, the proclaimer of good news, the Gospel. The Messiah had come, and she had talked to Him.

Back at Jacob's Well, the disciples had brought food for Jesus, but He wasn't hungry.

"Come on, Jesus. You have to eat something."

I have food that you don't quite understand, Jesus told them. He had just provided the water woman with living water, and she would never thirst again.

Jesus knew that the disciples wouldn't understand that He was providing spiritual food, like the water. It was a food that sustained but created a hunger for more.

Before long a crowd gathered. Spiritually hungry people, the rejected, the despised, came to Jesus with their preacher woman to learn more.

Beside Jacob's Well, Jesus began to teach about God, that He is a God of inclusion, not exclusion. Jesus told them that God loves Samaritans.

Does Jesus care?

Jesus talked to the Samaritans who were rejected by God's "chosen people." He told the Samaritans that they were God's children, too. Jesus traveled to Jacob's Well for a reason: to tell the rejected, the forbidden, the hopeless that they are God's children.

Does Jesus care? I know He cares.

Because He cared for a woman, one rejected by five husbands and by religious people, one who needed to know something important. She needed to know that she was not rejected by God.

This woman was the only person who could reach the lost, those who had lost hope. She became the mouthpiece of the Savior.

For two additional days, Jesus stayed and talked to Samaritans. The most excluded people of their day were hungry to learn more about God. Jesus stopped everything, went out of His way, to feed hungry souls beside a well.

Do you ever feel so excluded or rejected that you don't think anyone cares? Do you ever think that you have gotten so far away from God that even God does not care? Do you ever feel so rejected that not even God wants you?

Have you been rejected by love? Has someone ever told you they did not love you anymore? Having had the most intimate form of love, you were told that you were no longer loved. Have you been rejected by family? Have you been excluded by friends?

If there is ever a time in your life that you think that no one cares . . . well, Jesus cares.

Does Jesus care? Oh, yes, He cares! I know He cares!

He cares about the woman rejected by five husbands and by religion. He cares about the single mother who is struggling so hard to keep her life together. He cares about the elderly veteran who feels like he is a burden on his family and society.

He cares about the woman who spent nearly sixty years living in an iron lung.

He cares about the spouse who, for the first time in sixty-five years of marriage, is now alone.

Does anyone care? Does Jesus care?

How do I know?

He spent His life impacting people like you and me, who were at their lowest moments. He changed their lives, letting them know He cared.

Oh, yes, He cares. I know He cares. His heart is touched by my grief.

"Everyone who was willing and whose heart moved them came and brought an offering to the Lord for the work on the tent of meeting, for all its service, and for the sacred garments. All who were willing, men and women alike, came and brought gold jewelry of all kinds: brooches, earrings, rings, and ornaments."

—Exodus 35:21–22

CHAPTER TEN

Biltmore Mansion

When I was in college, I traveled with some friends to Asheville, North Carolina.

We arrived and saw Biltmore, the largest home ever built in America. It was on a gigantic, 8,000-acre farm.

The house is nearly 179,000 square feet, with 135,000 square feet of living space. It was built in 1889 by George Vanderbilt, who purchased over 500 parcels of land that included fifty farms and five cemeteries.

During construction, Vanderbilt installed a woodworking factory and a brick kiln that made 32,000 bricks a day. Work on building Biltmore required more than 1,000 workers and 60 stonemasons.

The home had more than 35 bedrooms, 43 bathrooms, and 65 fireplaces.

Finished in 1895 on Christmas Eve, it cost only $5 million—the equivalent of about $185 million today—but who had $5 million for a house back then? Most people were just pleased to have a house with a floor.

The Biltmore Estate is an extravagant American house, drawing more than 1.4 million visitors a year.

From the grandeur of Biltmore, we move to church buildings.

Generally, in America, a church is a church is a church. The building, that is. Most are nondescript. They have a meeting space/auditorium/sanctuary with classrooms. Usually there is a spire pointing up, perhaps with a cross on it.

That is true in the United States, but in visiting Israel, I found it to be a different world.

Stopping for lunch in a region called Beit Sahour, outside of Bethlehem, I walked into what had been the location of a beautiful church and monastery for centuries.

Part of the monastery has been renovated as a dining room; it is now a beautiful place for guests to eat. During lunch or dinner, your mind takes you back into what was once an active part of the church and monastery's daily life. Today, the proceeds from the restaurant support the maintenance of this beautiful place of worship.

The small cathedral is breathtaking! It is located on what was thought to be the shepherd's field where the birth of Christ was announced to the shepherds. While the building is a beautiful yet traditional design for a cathedral, the ceiling is absolutely, positively, unbelievable.

The ceiling's rich, dark blue brings attention to the multitude of stars in a late-night sky, complete with angels looking toward the ceiling's centerpiece: an image of Jesus holding the Word.

Having visited this site on two occasions, I am still amazed at the beauty of the church and the restoration of the monastery site.

There was a time when I had much to say about the use of

funds that it took to build beautiful cathedrals. The idea of using that much money on a building, a place of worship, seemed out of place, even a waste.

I now have a new respect for these amazing cathedrals. I used to use Judas's words when he criticized Mary as she was anointing our Lord with costly perfumes: "Such a waste! We could have sold that and fed the poor."

Why have I changed my mind about these amazing buildings? I looked at creation.

I re-examined what God has created for us. I reflected on a snowflake! When you closely look at a snowflake, you see extravagance. God created something as simple as frozen water and made an extravagantly beautiful snowflake. Some of our penny-pinching brethren might have made snow as a round flake. No extravagance.

Look at the makeup of the eye. We have the most amazing ability to see near or far. We can see when the light is dim or when the light is bright. The extravagance of the eye is an amazing gift from God.

Take something as simple as air. It is basically clear, except when light refracts through tiny drops of moisture suspended in the air, and then we have a bright explosion of beauty creating a rainbow! It's an amazing reminder of God's promise and God's extravagance.

The beauty of these churches is breathtaking! Workers spent most of their lives building and maintaining them. They were made to be beautiful for a reason.

When we look at the extravagance that God has shown to us through nature and His Word, we feel a need to begin to try to show the extravagance of our love to Him!

Why would I feel a need to criticize a group's effort to give back to God some of the glory He presented first to us? We are His most extravagant creation.

Moses asked the Israelites to contribute to build the Tabernacle, and they did.

They gave! They gave so extravagantly that Moses had to ask them to stop!

People of God were inspired by the powerful way that God brought them out of Egypt. The Israelites gave back out of overwhelming appreciation for His mighty acts.

In awe of the God of creation, people gave back extravagantly! Whether in their personal and private way or ever so extravagantly, people give back, trying, in a human way, to construct a place where they can worship the God of creation.

My travels took me to site after site in the Holy Land, where humans attempt to give back to our most generous Creator. Throughout the journey, one thing remained constant: the extravagance of the churches. They are beautiful works of art, like those expressions of the Israelites who built the Tabernacle and later Solomon's temple, all meant to reflect extravagance back to our Creator.

Imagine when we get to our eternal home—a home not built with hands but eternal in the heavens.

We are mere humans in awe of God's creation here. We even stand in awe of our own creation when we try to give some of the extravagance back to God. We will forever be amazed at what God is making for His children.

While we may criticize the cost of cathedrals, just think about the cost that God paid for us so that we can live in His eternal creation. It took His Son, our Savior.

Thanks be to God for His unspeakable, and extravagant, gift.

"He will carry the lambs in His arms, holding them close to His heart."

—Isaiah 40:11

CHAPTER ELEVEN

People

There are so many people who currently feel like they are . . .
Emotionally . . .
Physically . . .
Spiritually . . .
Mentally . . .
Figuratively . . .
Lost.
Standing on the edge, about to jump.

I have a friend who ran a center to help raped and abused women get away from the people who hurt them.

Not living in that world, I was unable to wrap my brain around an existence full of pain and fear.

My world was what I thought was typical: Mom, Dad, two kids, and a dog living in a simple house where we walked to our elementary school or rode the bus. My friends' homes were the same. That's just how America was, or so I thought.

We moved to the farm and also lived what I thought was typical family life there.

After school every day, we grabbed a bite to eat and worked on the farm with our dad. Mom would get home later and fix dinner, and then we'd watch TV or do stuff with our family.

My friend saw a different world. Her role was taking a mother and children out of an abusive home and putting them in secret living situations to protect them from violence . . . from the dad.

So unlike my world.

Another friend leads an effort to rescue women caught up in sex trafficking. The women are taken to a secure place to rehabilitate, and good people help them learn to live without the shroud of their abusers—criminals who did things like keep their victims holed up in hotels with drugs, abuse, and prostitution.

So unlike my world.

I had another friend who struggled with being gay and all that encompassed.

Years of fighting the fact that he was gay, trying to "pray the gay away," didn't work.

High school was rough, though not because of his friends. He was athletic and popular. The hardest part was coming home, where his being gay was a problem that divided his family. Dad didn't want him, while his mother tried to show her love.

Church was not a place of respite or support. Church leaders shared how they hated the sin—rejecting the "sinner."

He ended his life after a hurtful confrontation at home by speeding down a highway and heading directly into a tree.

Everywhere you look, there are so many who are going through . . .

Hard times . . .

Dark times . . .

Loveless times.

People are losing hope.

I want to implore you to see them. In the midst of crowds of people, they are there, standing on the edge of life and about to jump.

If you see someone on the edge, GRAB THEM.

Use both hands. Grab an arm. Grab a hand. Grab a leg. Grab anything you can reach.

Do it through a meal, or a phone call, or a letter, a Facebook message, a love offering, a smile, or a hug.

It doesn't matter how you do it. Let the Holy Spirit lead. But please reach out and grab them!

Grab them so they know that someone, somewhere, cares enough to hold them tight.

Imagine a world where there were no centers that helped rape and abuse victims. Few of us have the means to shelter abused women.

Thank God there are a few places that work hard to rescue desperate women from the sex trade. That work is messy. Thank God there are people willing to grab one weak soul who wants freedom and get them out of a cheap hotel room! That kind of person does not let go.

I do not understand churches that preach "hate the sin but love the sinner." It's never about greed or racism or adultery or problems we like to ignore.

Life gets hard, and people struggle. When you encounter them, never let them go.

We have hotlines for those struggling when no one grabs them. Perhaps they are fighting private battles. Those hotlines are there for those struggling alone, in hopes that some anonymous person can help them fight.

More than ever, children are fighting battles. Think back to your teenage years and remember how important some things were—being accepted or included. Those things seem so minor to us as adults, but they were crucial at that stage in life.

The children experiencing the problems of those teenage years touch our hearts. Kids commit suicide because of bullying or rejection. Kids in crisis often feel like no one understands them, and they consider suicide.

So grab them! Even if you don't understand their problems, hold on with all your heart.

When you see someone at a crossroads, help them find their way.

They may not be believers.

They may have made choices you can't imagine.

They may have been rejected for reasons that some other people or groups believe are fair.

Those who are rejected may think the outcast life is okay . . . until they need a community. They may find solitude preferable to the rejection they've been shown.

Or maybe they don't know how to ask God for help. Teach them. Show them there is hope.

The entire message of the Gospels—Matthew, Mark, Luke, and John—was to share a message of God's love for all mankind.

Jesus went to the sinners, the hungry, the broken who were on the ledge.

He embraced those who were rejected and hopeless. He taught us to do the same.

Imagine what life was like for the woman at the well. Do you think her home life was upper middle class with love and affection?

Perhaps her lifestyle was hard to love. There were five husbands.

Jesus sent His disciples away to buy food so He could deal with this broken, hurting woman who was probably doing what she could to survive. Her life was nowhere near perfect, but Jesus made a point to encounter her.

I think about the Man of the Gadarenes who lived in the cemetery. Talk about unloved and alone! The city put him in chains just to keep him away from "the good people." Jesus went out of His way to encounter the man . . . and save him from the ledge.

We have people just like these, struggling on their own.

It's easy to get lost, to wander away from those who love us . . . from God.

So when you find people wandering, bring them back.

Someone—spouse, family, or friend—already let them go. Your kindness, your ministry, could be the thread they follow back to a beautiful life.

Yes, it's easy to get lost. It's even easier to let people remain lost.

Not for Jesus.

Jesus does the opposite.

Jesus holds them, and you, tightly.

Just don't let go.

"He will carry the lambs in His arms, holding them close to His heart."—Isaiah 40:11

"By this all people shall know that you are my disciples, if you have love for one another."

—John 13:35

CHAPTER TWELVE

The Ties That Bind

Sometimes things just happen. Uneventful. Rather common. But very impactful.

There was an occasion when a White House news reporter, Sam Donaldson, and I were traveling together. Donaldson was known for pressing questions directed toward President Ronald Reagan.

He was the guest speaker at my alma mater, and I had the honor of bringing him to campus. On the way, Sam spent some time signing books for donors, as a thank you for their contributions.

As we traveled through rural West Tennessee, we talked of his battle with cancer. He shared a powerful story of diagnosis, treatment, and recovery. It was touching as he spoke of the fight.

I mentioned my friend Keith, who was also fighting cancer.

Keith and I attended college together. We were in a traveling, singing group and enjoyed our four-year experience. Keith and I also worked together at the university we attended. Development work. Alumni work. He was one of the best men I knew.

Keith had a tough fight with cancer and was losing hope.

Donaldson listened intently as I told him of Keith's struggle.

"Frank, do you have Keith's number? Can I call him?"

I was taken aback by his interest in Keith.

"You would be amazed by the new treatments and the progress that has been made in cancer treatment!" he told me. "Frank, Keith needs to hear this. Let me call him."

I called Keith and shared with him that Sam Donaldson and I were headed to campus and that Sam wanted to talk to him. Keith had difficulty accepting the fact that one of the most famous reporters in the country wanted to talk to him.

I handed the phone to Donaldson.

Sitting in the back of a limousine, I heard Donaldson share his struggle with cancer. He spoke passionately of new cancer trials that were life-changing. The conversation was not short. The conversation was not a courtesy.

Sam Donaldson had made a connection with someone he would never meet. Sam Donaldson made a connection with a fellow struggler with a life-threatening disease.

Two men became brothers that night.

Donaldson sharing his struggle at the most unexpected time touched Keith's heart, and he never forgot it.

The thoughtfulness of the gesture impressed me. Donaldson didn't have to do that, but he did.

Later that night, there was a standing ovation when the event was over. Donaldson had touched hearts. He exited the stage, shaking hands as he walked down the aisle to the lobby and then out to the waiting limo. More than three thousand people had heard his message of courage and inner strength.

As we drove to his hotel, Donaldson wanted to talk about Keith.

"Please encourage Keith and remind him that so much is being done in the fight against cancer," he said.

I thanked him for calling and talking to Keith.

As we approached his hotel, Donaldson shared how impressed he was with the university and the students. This semi-controversial news reporter pulled out the Bible that the students presented to him. The student body president had given him a Bible with signatures from the one thousand, four hundred students who were enrolled that year.

"I've never been given a gift that was this special. I will treasure this," he said.

I shared with him that he had visited a unique campus, with very impressive students. He agreed.

He and I exited the limo. We shook hands. He held up his new Bible and thanked me again for the experience, and I never saw him again.

I felt that something of the night touched him. Something connected with him. The evening had moved him.

Tonight, I did a similar thing, had another evening that was moving. A group of us get together kind of regularly, every other week or so. This night was special.

We ate dinner together, but it was different. We had our Thanksgiving dinner, but this wasn't just a Thanksgiving dinner. It was different and special because of who came to the table.

The conversation was normal: Tennessee football, the weather.

Some of the best people I know gathered in a kitchen and filled their plates with some of the season's best food. There was turkey, sweet potatoes, green bean casserole, broccoli casserole, sweet tea, congealed salads, and about four desserts. Around the table, we ate like kings. Our plates were full.

We went back for seconds. Then it happened. I'm sure it happens in other places. It happened tonight with about twelve or so of us.

There was an electrical engineer, a physician, a school administrator, a university professor, a pharmacist . . . the list goes on.

We laughed about fun things that happened when our "friends" pulled pranks in high school and college. Of course, we didn't pull any of those pranks: commodes on top of gyms, ponies in a dorm, cars picked up and placed in a dorm lobby.

We laughed, which made it uncomfortable for our full bellies.

Everyone could relate, which made it even funnier. Even though we would have NEVER participated in such pranks! Yeah, right.

We finished our meals, and the conversation changed to a subject that no one predicted. Those funny college stories began to slant to people and institutions that made powerful impacts on our lives. These stories all came back to the solid and most unchangeable parts of our lives.

Some of us were friends in college. Our lives have intertwined since those fun college days, and some were brought together by this group.

We have varied backgrounds. The conversation brought twelve people with varied backgrounds into one.

Amazing how we may have limited opportunities to interact with some people, but something clicks and a deep, meaningful relationship develops.

We had grown up all over the country. College was a common denominator for some, but not for most of the group. Everyone was talking about how others had come into their lives.

Who would have ever thought that a guy released from prison would impact someone's life in our group? His story did.

Who would have ever thought that the message from a friend who lost his wife would change lives? His story did.

No one anticipated that a father sharing the loss of a son, a son whom he still mourns, would impact lives this night. His story did.

A young lady who encountered a "wild child" had a life-changing experience. She never intended for a spark to develop. It did, and that "wild child" became one of the most stable men I know.

In each of these lives, something happened. Maybe something happened to you . . . probably unnoticed.

Looking at all these lives, one thing brought us together. And, over time, the stories changed each life.

Tonight, we experienced what I'm sure others have experienced. I've heard a term used before to describe such an encounter. When everything was over, and I was walking to the car, I was moved.

I don't know what was going on in any of the others' minds, but understanding was certainly going on in mine. As we all picked up our casserole dishes and headed to our cars, I wondered what others thought.

Sitting in the car, I understood how critical what we experienced is to life.

What we experienced was what others need. They want this connection deeply.

Every human being living today wants this: a relationship.

Relationships are hard.

You're new to a town, and you're trying to make friends.

Your child is new to school; one of their most critical needs is to make friends.

One of the most critical things to you is that your child makes the right kind of friends. I don't think that has as much to do with social standing as it does with making GOOD friends.

One of the hardest things to do is to develop good relationships. Every night, there are so many people who gather. This happens all over the country. This happens in other countries.

People gather to talk to their friend, a bartender, in a restaurant bar or a neighborhood bar.

They leave their houses or apartments to talk to their bartender.

Shoot, there was a TV show about it! They find in a bar what they have been unable to find in their communities. The bartender, if he is good, develops a trustworthy relationship with the customer for a reason.

People seek out relationships. We seek those who do not pass judgment. We seek those who do not yell at us. No one wants to be criticized.

People want to find acceptance. We develop subcultures to find acceptance for who we are.

Because people seek relationships. For divorced people, lives changed after a breakup. Families are divided over the people with whom they can associate. Because people seek relationships.

Recently, I was in a rural community and met with those who were trying to form a support group of like-minded people as they struggle through addictions. Because people seek relationships.

Young people having a difficult time developing relationships end up with similar young people in a gang. Because people seek relationships.

Tonight, as I sat in my car, it occurred to me that the twelve or so of us who gathered had what each subculture of our community wants. People seek relationships. They want to be with people who love them, support them, encourage them, and to feel like they're part of a group.

Tonight, I got to experience exactly what people want. There's a name for it. I've heard that name before. I've heard it used in other places.

Tonight, I experienced a thing. A thing called . . . "Church."

"Church" is a relationship.

There's a reason Christians call each other "brethren." It's "Church."

Paul said it correctly: "You were called into fellowship with His son . . ." It's "Church."

Once you find this relationship, it's addictive. Once you wrap your brain around this link, you want to share the connection.

The relationship lacks criticism, because there you find support. The connection lacks hate, because there you express love.

Tomorrow, there's coffee with a friend, a brother, someone who reached out to me several years ago, in love. What an impact he made in "Church."

Tomorrow, we'll talk and share and love.

It's not the first time, nor will it be the last. Interactions with him bring me closer . . . to Him.

Blessed be the tie that binds us.

"By this all people shall know that you are my disciples, if you have love for one another."

"For it is by grace you have been saved, through faith, and this is not from yourselves. It is the gift of God—not by works, so that no one can boast."

—Ephesians 2:8-9

CHAPTER THIRTEEN

Her Name Was Lucky

It was the evening of New Year's Day. At an interstate truck stop outside Jackson, Tennessee, someone had tied a small brown dog to a light pole amongst the tractor-trailer trucks.

In a bitterly cold, snowy night, a passerby spotted this helpless, short-haired dog shivering in the cold. Removing the dog from the leash, this person carried it inside where it was warm. A truck stop employee secured the frightened and freezing dog in a box in the employee break room.

At the end of her shift, she picked up the dog and carried it to her pickup and drove home. On January 2, she took the little brown dog to the Animal Care Center to be nursed back to health and placed up for adoption. In the meantime, it would go to a doggie foster home with one of my friends, who called me after getting the dog.

"Frank, when you have time, will you come over and let me show you something at my apartment?" she asked.

After work one day, I dropped by to see what she was talking about. We sat and talked a bit while her dogs roamed around her apartment. The conversation quickly went to dogs. Her dogs were so cute. Then the conversation became more personal.

"I know it was rough when Bonnie passed away. Have you ever thought about getting another dog?" she asked.

"Yeah, I have. I miss having a dog."

"Good, because I want you to take this little brown dog home and see if she 'fits' you."

I looked at the cute little dog, happy, content, sitting in my lap.

"I don't have any dog food for her."

"I have already bought a bag of dog food for her. It's there beside the door."

I looked at the door, and there was this large bag of dog food. "I take it that you bought that big bag of dog food in anticipation of me keeping that dog, didn't you?"

She grinned.

I carried the dog, and she carried the dog food as she told me the dog's story on New Year's Day.

I was touched. "I think I'll call her Lucky . . . Lucky Dog!"

That night, Lucky and I hit it off. How could I have gotten such a good dog, rescued from a harsh winter storm? I don't know. I was lucky, I guess.

When the lottery gets extremely high, people buy their lottery tickets. They begin to dream about what they will do if by chance they won the jackpot.

Lotteries have winners—sometimes huge winners, sometimes not so huge—but more than their dollar ticket costs them.

Why did they win? People will ask them: "How come you won? Was it the location? Did you have a secret formula for choosing the number?"

"Well, I guess I was just lucky."

No matter what happens, most people who survive a tornado or some other tremendous tragedy respond so similarly—whether they were inches from destruction or not injured at all.

"We were lucky. When the tornado came right at us, it destroyed our home. We were hunkered down in the center bathroom. We were lucky to have survived."

We live in a country that has difficulty in others being lucky.

We love it when we drive by an officer checking our speed. We see him and quickly step on our brake and hope that he didn't notice how fast we were going. We hope we were not going too fast!

We pass the officer and watch ever so carefully in our rearview mirror to see if he pulls out and turns his lights on. If he doesn't pull out, we feel sooooo lucky!

But let someone speed past us at a higher rate of speed, and we turn the corner and notice that the officer has pulled a car over . . . and it's the guy who passed us. "He got what was coming to him."

We want justice! We want everyone to get their just rewards! We want people to get what they deserve! Do the crime, do the time!

We want things to be fair. Yeah, we want things to be fair! Totally fair!

We even believe that God punishes the bad guys and rewards the good guys. Yeah, you do something bad, God zaps you!

Politicians and preachers often speak about this being a "Christian nation." God blesses this country because we are a "Christian nation."

Many believe that God is not blessing America! They believe that God is punishing America. Political campaigns rally people behind the idea that we're bringing a curse upon America because of sin. Scripture is even quoted.

"We must bring America back to God."

Yes, what a wonderful place it would be if our country's leaders would live by Christian principles.

I went to Africa to treat sick children, and it happened to be during our presidential election.

During that presidential campaign, I remember hearing that God was going to destroy our country because of a specific sin. We had to bring America back to God as a country.

When I landed in the country of Sierra Leone, Africa, I wondered what those people had done! Sierra Leone was a country of poverty, sickness, and despair.

What have these people done for God to punish them so harshly? I wondered. Country after country on this planet, living in poverty, absolute poverty, and I wondered . . . *what have these precious people done to be so cursed by God?*

We are so lucky that we have been born into such a righteous nation that God blesses us. God blesses the good and curses the bad . . . really???

Yeah, God gives people what they deserve! Right? We want God to be fair . . . right?

Read on.

This message has nothing to do with politics. This message has everything to do with God and who God is.

We now have Christian nationalism, with people believing that America is God's chosen people. They believe in combining politics and religion so God will bless America.

So back to this concept: God is fair. God is vengeful. God punishes people and countries who do bad things.

Stay with me here. Jesus talks about God and how He deals with people.

The Kingdom of God is like the man who started hiring people. Some began at eight in the morning. Then at ten, he hired some more people. Then at noon, he hired some more people. Then at four in the afternoon, he hired some more.

When it came time to pay the workers, the boss began to pay every worker the same amount!

What? Yes, he paid every worker the same amount!

Even though some worked all day long, and some only worked for one hour, they all got paid the same amount. Imagine how that conversation might have gone.

"That's not FAIR!" cried the guy who worked all day. "I worked all day in this hot sun, and that guy only worked for an hour, and he got the same amount that I did! We did the same work, but he only worked for an hour. That is not fair."

"Fair? What do you mean fair? Did you not agree to work for me starting at eight in the morning for this amount?"

"Yes."

"Did I pay you the amount that I agreed to pay you?"

"Yes, but you are going to pay that guy who worked an hour the same amount that you are paying me, even though I worked all day?"

"That's right."

"Why is he getting the same as me?"

"I guess he's just lucky."

We want everyone to get what's fair. We want everyone to get what they deserve. We want everyone to get their just reward.

Yes, that's what we want. We believe that God punishes the bad and rewards the good. That's how we think.

If that is what you want from Jesus . . . if that is what you expect from Jesus . . .

Then you're going to have a major problem with Jesus.

Life is not fair.

Read on.

Jesus taught: "Do you think that those eighteen people who died when the tower of Siloam fell were worse sinners than others?"

Again, from Jesus: "Do you think that the Galileans who suffered by Pilate when he mixed their blood with the sacrifices were any worse than others?"

What was Jesus trying to get across there? Jesus was making a point about life: It's not fair. People do not always treat you fairly.

Something happens to you that doesn't seem quite fair.

Cancer does not act fairly.

Car accidents happen so randomly. A tornado strikes your house and family but doesn't damage the house next door.

Maybe something happens to you that doesn't seem quite fair. You didn't get the promotion when you worked hard at being the best employee. You never win the prize, and you begin to feel like you are not deserving.

Oh, I believe that the person who works hard at being a better person, a good neighbor, a better worker, or a better spouse will be rewarded because that is how they live their life. Even then, life is not fair.

Many good things come because we work hard to achieve them.

I have a friend who runs. His running is an addiction. He loves it and looks forward to getting out and running no matter what the weather is like. One day, I was asking why running was so important to him.

"Frank, have you ever seen a runner smile?"

I had never thought about it. I don't typically look at runners' faces. They always seem to be running in their own little world.

"Frank, you never see a runner smile until you see him do something that he has prepared to do: run up some stairs.

"They have worked so hard in heat or rain or cold. You see them smile when others frown, like on the stairs. They can run upstairs like you did when you were young. Frank, that's when you see a runner smile."

A runner prepares for marathons, 5Ks, or stairs. They put their lives on a trajectory so that at some point they reap a benefit.

I get that. Sometimes we get something because we work for it. This is totally different.

Understand that Jesus was radical for His day. He taught

differently from the scribes and Pharisees. Jesus had a radical message; perhaps you have noticed that. He taught differently.

Jesus was in the temple on the Sabbath when an older woman walked in and was bent over. She had lived that way for eighteen years of her life.

Jesus called her to him. Jesus spoke to her, then put his hands on her, and her body straightened up.

What did she do to be bent over like that? Had God punished her?

What did she do to be healed? What did she do that she deserved to be healed? Did she get what she deserved?

Was she like blind Bartimaeus, crying out, "Jesus, Son of David, have mercy on me?" Nope.

Did she push her way through the crowd trying to touch the hem of His garment to be healed? Nope.

Did she get her friends to find where Jesus was and get them to lower her through the roof of the house to be healed? Nope.

Did she say, "I have faith. Only speak the word, and I'll be healed?" Nope.

What did she do? She was simply at the right place at the right time.

She got lucky.

The only thing she could claim was that she was **THERE**. Jesus was teaching at the synagogue, and she was there. She just showed up. She got lucky simply by being there.

Probably in His radical manner, Jesus taught His disciples about what we call the Beatitudes. He probably meant:

Lucky are the poor in spirit (humble), because now they **HAVE** the Kingdom of Heaven.

Lucky are those who mourn, because they **NOW** have a comforter.

Lucky are the meek (those with self-control), because they will **NOW** inherit the Earth.

Lucky are those who hunger and thirst for righteousness, because they can NOW be filled, filled here and now with teaching that you cannot find with the scribes and Pharisees.

Lucky are the merciful, because they can NOW receive God's pure mercy.

Lucky are those who have pure hearts, because NOW they can look upon God.

Lucky are the peacemakers, because they are NOW my children.

Lucky are those who are persecuted because they are living right; they NOW have the Kingdom that God has promised throughout eternity.

This is a hard message for many of us to grasp. We seem to be consumed with the idea of God punishing us . . . zapping us.

I assume that you are reading this and that you are a believer. As such, you believe in grace.

You're really, really lucky.

Did you do anything to deserve God's grace? Of course not. You're just a believer.

You are like the woman who was bent over when Jesus met her in the synagogue. You were lucky to have had an encounter with Jesus, and because you were convinced that He was the Christ, God in the flesh.

For by grace are we saved—not because of what we have done, but by simply understanding who He is.

You sure are lucky that you encountered Jesus. Make sure you help others encounter Him as well.

Go live your life in peace, because you are a child of God . . . a child of the King.

> "Give, and it will be given to you.
> A good measure, pressed down, shaken together
> and running over, will be poured into your lap.
> For with the measure you use,
> it will be measured to you."
>
> —Luke 6:38

CHAPTER FOURTEEN

How Shall I Be Remembered?

When I was a young man in my hometown of Columbia, an elderly woman living in a large house with an overgrown yard passed away.

My uncle owned a jewelry store on West Seventh in downtown Columbia. The woman lived on West Sixth Street, not far from his store. His friends on the police force kept him informed about what was found in the house.

After her death, folks shared a lot of stories about this unique neighbor, like how she never let people into her home. Fencing blocked off the house, preventing easy access. Delivery guys talked about bringing her groceries.

Evidently, her mattresses were full of cash. The house was

filled with so much stuff that it was difficult to move from room to room. Her garage had classic cars that had not been driven in decades.

Today, the house and its owner are gone, but her story lives on.

There was another woman I will never forget. I was in my office working on something that had to be very important—so important that I don't remember what it was. What I do remember, however, was the elderly lady who walked in and sat down. I had known her since I was a teenager; I was now president of our Christian school.

We talked about the weather. We talked about stuff I did when I was a kid. Finally, there was a lull in the conversation, that kind of quiet when you don't know what to do or say.

She became a little emotional. I knew she was going to say something. She had lost her husband a couple of years earlier. They were such a wonderful couple. Then she broke the silence, "Frank, I want my name to be on something other than a tombstone."

I didn't know how to respond. I was thirty-two years old and talking to the sweetest woman. She had watched me grow up. I didn't know where to go with this statement of hers.

"I hear that the school is building a grandstand for football games. I have never been to a football game. My husband loved watching football games. I never understood it."

I walked over to the large window and invited her to look out at the football field.

"The grandstand on that field needs replacing," I said.

She shared how she loved the school and what good it was doing for the next generation of kids.

She walked back to her chair. I sat in the chair next to her and didn't say a word. I was a little confused. She didn't watch football. She didn't even understand football.

With tears in her eyes, she began, "Frank, I have had the most blessed life. We were never able to have children, but we have always loved them. Tell me what I can name and how much it would cost?"

My heart melted. I will never forget that day.

We live in the most prosperous nation in the history of the Earth. We have been so blessed. We live in the best homes, drive the nicest cars, eat the best food, and have the safest water. We have people who risk their lives trying to get into our country. They are happy to get the lowest-paid jobs available, jobs we don't want to do, in order to be safe and to provide for their families.

Our neighborhoods are safe, and our children are taught by excellent teachers. We are able to exceed our parents' wildest dreams.

With all the strength of the Spirit, I believe this message from God, "Give and it will be given to you. A good measure, pressed down, shaken together, and running over, will be poured into your lap."

There is something in that message from God that we overlook: Giving is good for you!

The God who created and holds the world in place has stated that whatever the amount you give, God blesses you so much more in return. The return on the gift is greater for you than for whoever received the gift.

Some of you don't believe that. *No,* you think, *you preachers and you fundraisers just want more money. It's all about the money.*

No, it's not about the money. It's about God.

God knows what makes us be better people. God knows that we are better people when we give time, talents, and resources.

I am a better human when I help the poor have food. This gives me perspective about the blessings that I have.

I am a better human when I give my time to encourage those losing hope. Humanity is better served when we try to rescue those who have lost heart, thus losing their way.

I am a better human when I financially support causes that are good for the Kingdom and the community. Then I take ownership of and express the importance of both, because we live in both worlds.

It's more than money or time. We are being more like God.

"God loves a cheerful giver."

"Give, and it will be given back to you."

"Command them to do good, to be rich in good works, to be generous and ready to share . . . so that they may take hold of that which is truly life," says 1 Timothy 6:18.

What God has promised has always been true.

In Malachi, the Lord says, "Bring the whole tithe into the storehouse and test me and see. I will throw open the floodgates of Heaven and pour out so much blessing that there will not be room enough for it."

Giving changes your life because giving impacts your heart.

The apostle Timothy tells us we are to do good, to be rich in good works, to be generous and ready to share.

In those early years of our country, every college that started in America had a spiritual motive and was built with gifts from God's people.

Taking care of orphans and widows has always been the mission of God's people, who were giving from their heart to help the most vulnerable.

But how shall I be remembered?

There comes a time that you begin to see the end of life. It's down the road, sometimes far off, sometimes rather close, but you have the end in view.

When you die, people will come to your funeral. And as much as they loved you, the attendance around your open grave will depend on the weather. The memories of your funeral will soon be forgotten.

So how shall I be remembered?

I have yet to hear people talk about the size of a tombstone and be impressed.

The purpose of this writing is to ask you to go one step further: Prepare for life as you prepare to leave this world.

When I ask how you will be remembered, my purpose is to help you reflect on the impact you are making on those around you—namely God's people.

The best people in the world, those who have Kingdom eyes, those who see beyond this world and into the next generation, how shall you be remembered?

I have noticed that some get grumpy about what they see around them. They don't get along with their neighbor. They seem to be highly critical of their preacher, or the president. They look at young people who sit in the back row at church or gather and hang out at parks or parking lots.

Often, you will be remembered by how you view others.

How shall I be remembered?

Ira North, who preached for decades at a huge church in Madison, Tennessee, often came to my hometown when I was a teenager. The things he said, I have never forgotten.

"I would love to drive into a city and stop and ask, 'Who in this city feeds the poor?'"

"Oh, you don't know?"

"Who in this city helps meet the needs of the elderly?"

"Oh, you don't know?"

"Who in this city helps those who are struggling?"

"Oh, you don't know? Well, you must not be from around here. We thought everyone knew that around here, God's people care for all of His children as they struggle."

How shall you be remembered?

Your life will determine how you will be remembered.

How you love. How you care. How you share.

It's not that hard. Enjoy the blessings that come back to you out of the goodness of our loving God.

"Suppose one of you has a hundred sheep and loses one of them. Doesn't he leave the ninety-nine in the open country and go after the lost sheep until he finds it? And when he finds it, he joyfully puts it on his shoulders and goes home."

—Luke 15:4-6

CHAPTER FIFTEEN

Whoever, Wherever, Whatever

On a healing trip to Africa, we were in a tiny village in the middle of nowhere you would know. We arrived in this quiet village and requested permission from the tribal chief to treat sick children.

Malaria, diarrhea, and respiratory infections kill many children in Africa. We were trying to make a difference.

Within an hour, the small village became overwhelmed with moms hearing that healers were there to treat their sick children. Word traveled fast because the need was great for someone to heal their children.

The tribal chief was grateful for our visit. Our physician was one of their own. While working in Jackson, this doctor saved everything he could to purchase medicine to treat the sick in his home country of Sierra Leone, Africa.

There once was another healer who came to save His people.

While Jesus was not attempting to be famous, He became the hottest ticket in the Middle East. People began to follow Him.

Fathers with dying children, the lame and broken, the lepers, and the blind came to Him for healing. Followers with all kinds of maladies came and were healed, then stayed to hear about the coming Kingdom that had been prophesied for generations.

Time and time again, people came to be healed but stayed for the sermon.

After seeing someone healed, those witnesses were filled with awe. News spread throughout the region, and great crowds followed Him and brought their sick.

The sick, lame, and broken came to be healed, and they found a healer from God.

Before long, the opposition began to accuse Jesus of healing by the power of Satan: "He heals by the power of Beelzebul."

The opposition couldn't deny the miracle, so they denied the power by which Jesus healed.

How did the people respond? The people ignored those religious leaders and continued to bring their sick.

Then late one night, one of the religious leaders came to Jesus and acknowledged His holiness: "No one can do these things unless that person is sent by God."

In Jesus's time, what stronger confirmation could He receive other than for a Pharisee to sneak away to talk to Him about His mission, ministry, and message?

During the primitive medical times of the first century, to have someone make the blind see, make the lame walk, and raise the dead meant that Jesus was such a hope to those suffering.

Using healing to gather the crowds and create awe and confirmation that the message was from God, Jesus the Savior began to treat sin as an illness. Sin was a therapeutic issue. A sinner is sick and needs a physician. A sinner needs a doctor—one who treats with mercy.

Don't leave me here; keep reading.

Jesus was showing what the Kingdom of God looks like . . . like a leper being cleansed and healed and then welcomed home.

Can you imagine, having lived so long away in leper colonies, being cleansed from leprosy and returning home to be welcomed back into the family?

Imagine the blind and lame returning home, healed and ready to be a productive member of the family. What a homecoming!

Imagine those possessed by a demon being set free and returning to the family, cleansed and free!

Imagine the woman who had been sick for years, who was healed by merely touching the hem of His garment. She could return home able to love on her children and family where before, her illness prevented her from having a normal life.

Imagine the widow who was following the funeral parade for her only son when she encountered Jesus. Imagine that grand reunion, after the horrible death of her child, when Jesus gave him back to her. Or imagine the father who sought Jesus's help as his little girl lay dying, only to get the news that she had passed before they reached her. Imagine the family celebrating when Jesus brought their child back to life.

Jesus the healer, sharing the Good News.

Jesus the healer, telling His twelve: "Proclaim the Good News, 'The Kingdom of Heaven has come near.' Heal the sick, raise the dead, cleanse those who have leprosy, and drive out demons."

And that they did.

Peter and John healed at the Beautiful Gate. Peter and Paul raised the dead. Paul did so after he preached too long, and a boy sitting in a window fell asleep, slipped off the windowsill, and died.

We should feel the need to do what the apostles did and become agents of healing. Yes, we should become agents of healing and known as agents of healing.

Our Christian world has become full of those who push the socially sick away and condemn the sick: *I'll have nothing to do with that social leper!*

In our country, there are many self-righteous who push the sick away, removing themselves from what they are called to be. Instead of being healers, many have become the Pharisees of our day, keeping people from Jesus and His healing power.

Back to the purpose of this message: us as healers. I have been sent out as a healer, just as you have been. By the power of Jesus, we are sent to carry the medicine of mercy and become agents of healing as we gather at clinics of grace.

Our world is fighting a culture war—a war that is not good and definitely not encouraged by God. We live in a world of culture war crusaders when God calls us to become agents of healing.

Do we carry the condemning message of the crusaders or one of mercy from the Healer?

Are we sent to inflict pain and hate on sinners or to carry the message that restores and returns the sick to a loving home?

Our world is mean, but we should be kind, because God calls us to love. Our world is divided, yet we should be united, because we are His family. Our world has many Pharisees who create a show by spewing hate, when God gathers the hurting and creates healing.

Throughout history, we had crusades and inquisitions—none of which were ever blessed by God—where the goals were killing people and burning witches and heretics.

At times, God's people did bad things in His name, thinking that He justified them. People still do. God's people spew hate toward entire segments of the population, telling us to hate them because of their race, nationality, class, or other station in life. The latest targets are those who are born gay.

Creating hate is not what God ever called a Christian to do. Condemning the socially sick is not what God ever instructed followers to do. God's people are missionaries of mercy, carrying the medicine of mercy and love.

God's message has never changed. God tells us to love. God's instructions have never changed: Love one another. As a follower of God, you have never been instructed to condemn, but you *have* been instructed to love.

It cannot be more beautifully stated: "The Word became flesh and made His dwelling among us. We have seen His glory, the glory of the one and only Son, who came from the Father, full of grace and truth."

God did not send His Son into the world to condemn the world, but so that the world, through Him, might have life.

The world is full of those who are sick, and again, we are the missionaries of mercy.

My first visit to the church where I worship, I heard the strangest thing. I had never heard a church say these words and mean it.

"Whoever you are, wherever you have been, whatever you have done, you are welcome here."

I heard that and said, "This church doesn't believe that. That minister doesn't really mean that."

He did.

So I posted it on social media each Sunday, and it wasn't long before a guy sent me a message: "I am here. I drove from Nashville to worship here."

He came because of that one statement. He came back to worship again. He came back again, to worship at a place where sinners were welcome to hear a message of God's love.

On his third visit, he said, "I can't keep driving here from Nashville to worship. I'll try to find this kind of church in Nashville."

Then there was a message from a lesbian couple: "Would we be welcome there?"

I reached out to leadership and asked.

Word came back: "How can we exclude anyone from worshiping with people who love God and want to know more about that love?"

If you are reading this, just know that God will never reject you.

He left the ninety-nine and found the one who wandered away.

Jesus spent an entire night to get to one man who lived in a cemetery, rejected by his community.

Jesus told the story of the prodigal son who was welcomed home.

Whoever you are, even if you've been rejected, you're welcome with God's people.

Wherever you are, you're welcome to come home to be with God's people.

Whatever you've done, you'll find that God's people are full of mercy and grace . . . even if we don't deserve it.

Jesus came to heal the sick. We are here to help you with the healing power of the love of God.

He will not reject you. He will forgive you. He's your healer. He's your savior.

You're the child of a King. Come claim your inheritance.

Dr. Frank McMeen

For more than two decades, Dr. Frank McMeen has been president of the Community Foundation of West Tennessee (formerly known as the West Tennessee Healthcare Foundation) in Jackson, Tennessee. He is a former vice president of university advancement at Freed-Hardeman University, a past president of Columbia Academy, and he was an adjunct faculty member at the University of Memphis and Freed-Hardeman University. He has served as president of the Lambuth Area Neighborhood Association off and on for more than ten years, and he was elected to Jackson's City Council. He serves on numerous boards, including the Boys & Girls Club, Jackson Equity Project, and Jackson Rotary Club. He is treasurer of the Tennessee Dental Association Foundation and was president of the Association for the Preservation of Tennessee Antiquities. He received the 2012 Outstanding Alumnus Award from the University of Memphis Alumni Association for the University College Chapter. He was named Jackson's 2023 Man of the Year.

He enjoys historic preservation and is restoring his thirteenth historic home in Jackson. He loves animals and rescued his dogs, Bonnie May, Lucky Dog, and Minnie Mutt. He worships at Skyline Church. He was raised on a farm outside Columbia, Tennessee, where walking horses were a vital part of his life, with his father winning two world grand championships.

Your Life Is a Story: God Loves Every Page of Your Life is McMeen's third book. His previous books include *Let Me Tell You a Story: Finding Hope in a Hopeless World* and *It's All about a Story: Be Encouraged*.

www.ingramcontent.com/pod-product-compliance
Lightning Source LLC
Chambersburg PA
CBHW040234110526
44582CB00002B/46